Museum Development and Cultural Representation

Museum Development and Cultural Representation critically examines the development of a museum and cultural heritage centre in the indigenous Kelabit Highlands in Sarawak, Malaysia.

Building on their direct involvement in the development of the project, the authors appraise the process in retrospect through a thematic analysis. Themes covered include the project's local and international contexts, community involvement and agency, the balance of tourism and authenticity, and the role of non-local partners. Through their analysis, the authors unpack the complexities of cultural representation and identity in heritage design practice, and investigate the relationship between capacity building and agency in cultural heritage management.

Situating the project within international trends in museology, *Museum Development and Cultural Representation* offers a valuable case example of a heritage-making process in an indigenous community. It will be of interest to scholars and students studying cultural representation, as well as communities and museum professionals looking to develop similar projects.

Jonathan Sweet is a researcher and teacher of Museology, Cultural Heritage and Development at Deakin University, Australia.

Meghan Kelly is Senior Lecturer in Visual Communication Design at Deakin University, Australia, and currently serves as the Associate Head of the School for Teaching and Learning in the School of Communication and Creative Arts.

Museum Development and Cultural Representation
Developing the Kelabit Highlands Community Museum

Jonathan Sweet and Meghan Kelly

LONDON AND NEW YORK

First published 2019
by Routledge

2 Park Square, Milton Park, Abingdon, Oxfordshire OX14 4RN
52 Vanderbilt Avenue, New York, NY 10017

Routledge is an imprint of the Taylor & Francis Group, an informa business

First issued in paperback 2020

Copyright © 2019 Jonathan Sweet and Meghan Kelly

The right of Jonathan Sweet and Meghan Kelly to be identified as authors of this work has been asserted by them in accordance with sections 77 and 78 of the Copyright, Designs and Patents Act 1988.

All rights reserved. No part of this book may be reprinted or reproduced or utilised in any form or by any electronic, mechanical, or other means, now known or hereafter invented, including photocopying and recording, or in any information storage or retrieval system, without permission in writing from the publishers.

Notice:
Product or corporate names may be trademarks or registered trademarks, and are used only for identification and explanation without intent to infringe.

British Library Cataloguing-in-Publication Data
A catalogue record for this book is available from the British Library

Library of Congress Cataloging-in-Publication Data
A catalog record for this book has been requested

ISBN: 978-1-138-55435-1 (hbk)
ISBN: 978-0-367-60674-9 (pbk)

Typeset in Times New Roman
by Apex CoVantage, LLC

Contents

List of figures	vi
About the authors	vii
Acknowledgements	viii
List of abbreviations	ix

1	A unique cultural museum	1
2	Shaping Kelabit conservation processes in Southeast Asia	19
3	History, knowledge and the representation of identity	32
4	Museum development and tourism: identifying authenticity and representation	45
5	Indigenous knowledge in community museum practice	57
6	Shaping the discussion on conservation	70
7	The development of the Kelabit Highlands Community Museum	81
8	Detailed encounters	95
9	Concluding remarks	114
	Index	126

Figures

1.1	Location of Bario in Sarawak, East Malaysia, Meghan Kelly, 2018	6
6.1	Stone Monolith, Kelabit Highlands, June 2012	78
8.1	Kelabit Highlands Community Museum Development Plan 2012	99
8.2	Community consultation notes, Miri, January 2014	103
8.3	Architecture student concepts, January 2014	106
8.4	Construction drawings by Lian Tarawe, 2015	109
8.5	Kelabit Highlands Community Museum under construction, December 2015	109
8.6	Interpretive material, Visual Communication Design Fieldwork, December 2015	111
8.7	Exhibition in the Kelabit Highlands Community Museum, Bario	112

About the authors

Jonathan Sweet is a researcher and teacher of museology, cultural heritage and development at Deakin University, Australia. He is a graduate of the Royal College of Art in the History of Design and has a PhD in history and museology. He has participated as a Chief Investigator on a number of Australian Research Council grants. Amongst his publications are contributions to the journals, *South East Asia Research* (2006) and *Museum and Society* (2014), the *Handbook of Research on Development and Religion* (Edward Elgar 2013) and the *Oxford Handbook of Public History* (2017). He maintains strong connections with colleagues in South and Southeast Asia: he has acted as an advisor to UNESCO and to ICCROM; worked in partnership with academics at the University of Calcutta and been a Visiting Honorary Fellow at the Postgraduate Institute of Archaeology, University of Kelaniya, Sri Lanka.

Meghan Kelly is a Senior Lecturer in Visual Communication Design at Deakin University and currently serves as the Associate Head of School for Teaching and Learning in the School of Communication and Creative Arts. Kelly's research explores issues surrounding identity creation and representation in a cross-cultural context with a focus on indigenous communities. Kelly co-authored the Australian and International Indigenous Design Charters (2016), best practice documents for designers working with indigenous knowledge in commercial communication design. As a practicing visual communication designer, Kelly's experience includes the advertising and design industries and running her own design studio. Kelly is a member of the Design Institute of Australia (DIA) and the International Council of Design (ico-D).

Acknowledgements

We would like to acknowledge the contribution of the late Jaman Ribuh, an inspirational participant in the KHCMDP.

Rurum Kelabit Sarawak
Deakin University Faculty of Arts and Education
Deakin International

Abbreviations

AIPP	Asia Indigenous People Pact
BN	Barisan Nasional
ICCROM	The International Centre for the Study of the Preservation and Restoration of Cultural Property
ICOM	International Council of Museums
DU	Deakin University
KHCMPD	Kelabit Highlands Community Museum Project Development
RKS	Rurum Kelabit Sarawak
UNESCO	The United Nations Educational, Scientific and Cultural Organization

1 A unique cultural museum

Introduction

In recent years, a key stream of enquiry into the dynamics of cultural heritage and museum studies in the countries of Asia has been focused on understanding the relationships between conservation and cultural representation.[1] Many of these countries were created through a process of decolonisation, and their citizens are of diverse origins and ethnicity. This has raised the question of the extent to which these nations have been able to accommodate diversity within the idea of a unified nation state. In an effort to address the problem of inclusion, cultural heritage agencies and conservation practitioners have considered how best to incorporate concepts such as human rights, cultural diversity, indigenous knowledge and notions of authenticity into their activities. This has been of critical importance to the evaluation of the processes that have shaped heritage conservation and cultural representation in the region.[2] In this book, we document and contextualise a museum development in Malaysia that engages with these important issues. Discourse has been developed by taking a case study approach to explore the historical, political, religious and cultural issues and processes that have influenced the development of a community museum by the non-Malay indigenous Kelabit people of Sarawak, Malaysian Borneo.

The Routledge Handbook of Heritage in Asia[3] drew attention to the relationships between global, national and local approaches to heritage conservation and the priorities of government policies. More broadly, this discourse has enhanced the understanding of how concepts of heritage have been incorporated into development programs and influenced conservation practices and outcomes. It has shown that in many parts of Asia centralised government conservation policies and processes have often neglected ethnic, religious and indigenous communities. For example, at the UNESCO World Heritage Sites *The Town of Luang Prabang*, in Laos PDR, and *The Mountain Resort and its Outlying Temples, Chengde*, in Hebei Provence,

China, 'the outstanding universal significance' of these places may have been very narrowly defined to reflect the ideological interests of their governments.[4] As an early observer of conservation processes in Asia, Dennis Burn noted the process of determining heritage significance grew from a largely western conservation perspective. Essentially these countries 'followed the West in using ancient monuments and sites as iconic emblems of nation'.[5] This means that they often failed to incorporate the local and spiritual complexity of historic sites and cultural landscapes. In this book, we develop the discourse by looking at the issue of inclusion from another perspective, which is to understand the particular circumstances and processes through which a marginalised community in Malaysia have pursued the conservation of their tangible and intangible cultural heritage interests with very little government patronage.

In Malaysia, economic development policies and priorities have compromised the conservation of heritage of significance to ethnic, religious or indigenous minorities.[6] When seen from a human rights perspective, these instances of neglect or deliberate exclusion from government decision-making processes reflect a broader concern in the region that has fuelled the argument that the values of local communities ought to be respected and local people ought to have agency in the conservation of their own heritage. At the highest level, the association between heritage and human rights is affirmed in the ratification of United Nations (UN) conventions, while in practice the principles and obligations enshrined in these conventions may be compromised in pursuit of national interest. In the 1995 Declaration on Cultural Diversity, the United Nations Education Scientific and Cultural Organisation (UNESCO) warned that 'development divorced from its human or cultural context is growth without a soul'.[7] Nevertheless, despite the rhetoric in support of social inclusion, some ethnic, religious or indigenous minority communities have continued to find their values undermined by development while, in tourism policies, heritage conservation may have been integrated into economic development. As a result, marginalised communities are unlikely to have achieved transformative rewards because the programs are often developed within a centralised system.[8]

The Kelabit people of Sarawak are an ethnic, religious and indigenous minority community who have sought to progress their agency in the management of their cultural heritage assets. As anthropologist Sarah Hitchener observed in 2009, the Kelabit people 'are designing and managing their own projects aimed at cultural revitalization and documentation of their cultural heritage'.[9] There are various reasons for their activities, which are discussed in this book, but in part, the proactive attitude adopted by the Kelabit people has responded to the ways in which the national government has misunderstood or narrowly defined the concept of 'cultural heritage' and the relationship that heritage has with identity. The recent formation of the state of Malaysia in 1963 meant that there has been a strong desire to correlate government cultural policy with the construction of national identity. The roots of this lie in the process of decolonisation, where, according to historian Tan Tai Yong, there was 'little historical basis' for creating the nation state of Malaysia:

> the making of Malaysia . . . represented state-formation on quite an ambitious scale. It essentially entailed the integration of four distinct entities – in terms of historical development, ethnic makeup, and varying stages of political and economic development – into a single unified nation-state.[10]

The challenges of unification were evident in East Malaysia (Sarawak and Sabah), where the relations of the former British colonies with their neighbour Brunei were subject to deep-seated 'religious, territorial, ethnic and historical animosities' that were 'compounded by a reluctance to share oil wealth'.[11] Thus, cultural heritage policy and associated development programs grew out of a need to find a way to bring cohesion to the federation of so-called Malay states and came to be seen as a way to assist with the construction of national identity. Museums in Malaysia have had an important role in this process. Abu Talib Ahmad has observed that since the introduction of a national culture policy in 1971, museums have effectively been instruments of the government, and they have been used predominately to promote Malay Muslim values. He has argued that in presenting these narratives to the public, there have been notable 'exclusions and silences', because these represent alternative views that were designated as 'politically or religiously incorrect'.[12] In other words, in Malaysia, the idea of 'cultural heritage' has been interpreted as a very specific reference to Malay Muslim values, and the state museums are effectively used as propaganda arms of the national government.

The Kelabit Highlands Community Museum Development Project (KHCMDP) emerged as a response to this exclusionary context. We argue that the Kelabit community have viewed the museum project as a means to conceptualise and frame an integrated strategy for the conservation of Kelabit heritage values and to assist with the reintegration of their cultural heritage and identity, which had been fractured by their circumstances since WWII. The project provided a process to reflect on the deeper relationships between the distant and recent pasts and their contemporary circumstances, as well as an opportunity to increase agency in the management of culture for their own social and economic development. Abu Talib Ahmad may be correct to argue that the national cultural policy introduced by the

Malaysian government has 'been under siege by non-Malay groups ever since its inception'.[13] Nevertheless, the project should not be viewed too shallowly as a muscular expression of cultural resistance, as there is much evidence that the Kelabit people have for a number of generations effectively engaged with various social and political processes to progress their own cultural interests. Thus, the book shows that the museum development project reflects a far more complex coalescence of intellectual and cultural activities, and that the analysis of the project affords us an opportunity to extend our understanding of how an ethnic, religious and indigenous minority in Southeast Asia is redefining the idea and purposes of the community museum to suit their own needs.

Cross-cultural action research

The KHCMDP was undertaken between 2011 and 2016, and this book provides an account of the project. The narrative and analysis were focused on the background and the processes through which the Kelabit museum was conceptualised and realised. The book therefore contributes an insight into the history and culture of the contemporary Kelabit people as well as into a broader understanding of the processes through which people belonging to non-Malay indigenous minorities in Malaysia are seeking to achieve greater agency in the conservation and representation of their cultures.

The creation of the museum was a significant intellectual project that was owned by the Kelabit people of Sarawak, but this book has been written from a western academic perspective. While the authors were involved as consultants in the conceptualisation and development of the museum, this account may be criticised for being yet another outcome of a neo-colonial or paternalistic relationship. However, such a criticism would greatly underestimate the intelligence and competencies of the Kelabit leadership and the pride and resilience of the local community. In effect, the authors were participants in a cross-cultural research process, and throughout their association with the Kelabit community they remained deeply cognisant of a range of issues concerning the relationships between the representatives of the Kelabit people, the authors and their associates.[14]

The research was pursued through a process of participatory action research, which was focused on understanding and interpreting the circumstances and mechanisms of change through which the Kelabit community embraced their responsibility for the conservation and representation of their culture. At the centre of this knowledge exchange between the participants were formal and informal discussions and activities that addressed the conservation and representation of heritage places, things and values, and discussed how these might be integrated into the community museum concept. The ideas and activities that were contributed by the authors of this book were theorised with reference to local circumstances and the discourses of museology, cultural heritage conservation and cultural representation through film, architecture and visual communication design. From the community's perspective, these discussions were permeated with a combination of strategic management and heartfelt emotion, and infused with attitudes shaped through historical and political events, religious beliefs and the cultural practices that the community had experienced since WWII.

An engagement with modernity has deeply influenced the attitudes of the Kelabit people towards safeguarding their culture from further erosion. Their actions in facilitating the development of the museum were certainly driven by the perceived need to act quickly to address some pressing issues, for example, the loss of their own language. The book therefore provides an account of a heritage conservation project where the focus was on the process of developing a community museum. The starting point was the discussion within the Kelabit community about the possibilities of how museological and/or technological ideas and methods could benefit conservation and social development, and the way in which this might be achieved. The project therefore can also be characterised as an example of cultural and economic development, which included 'heritage-making'. This means that the adoption of various methodologies required some consensus in the articulation and prioritisation of heritage places, things and values. Naturally, this revealed some tensions and diversities of opinion, which are discussed here. Nevertheless, throughout the project the Kelabit people addressed the conservation of their cultural heritage through a range of activities that included defining their heritage places, things and values. They discussed and initiated ideas for the ways in which these were to be interpreted, and in some instances to be given a visible form.

In this account, the project is contextualised historically through explaining the community's comparatively recent experiences of the processes of decolonisation that began at the end of WWII. Because they are a non-Malay indigenous ethnic group, this has included understanding how experiences of indigenousness, Christianity and modernity have been ingested into the values and expressions of the community. Unravelling this complexity in the history of the Kelabit people is essential to understanding the consultative approach taken to the conservation of their cultural heritage. In addition, the close inspection of the process of development means that the book is also able to contribute information to the discourse of community development through a discussion of the tools of action research and community consultation that were used in the museum development project. This includes understanding the roles of leadership, cross-cultural and/or transnational relationships and community participation in these specific

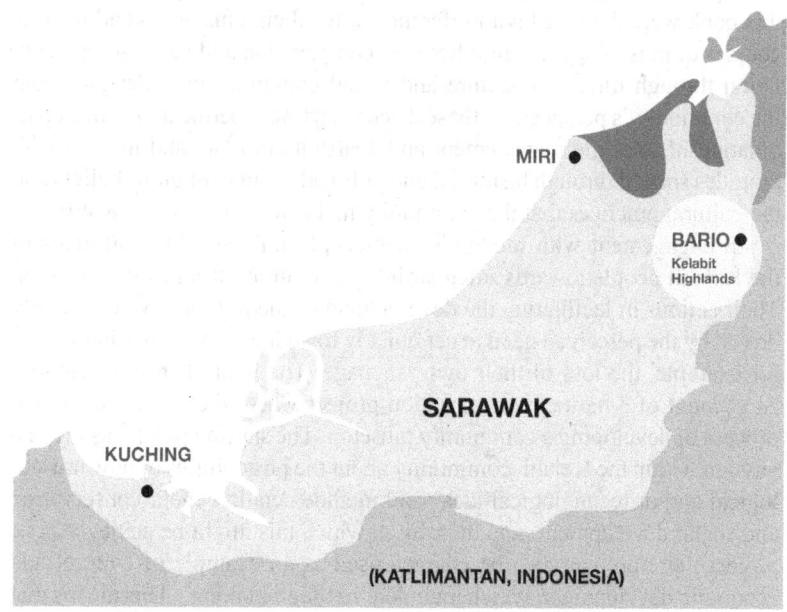

Figure 1.1 Location of Bario in Sarawak, East Malaysia, Meghan Kelly, 2018

circumstances. In all, this book provides an insight into the processes through which community-based heritage conservation and cultural representation are being pursued in Southeast Asia – primarily through negotiation between local and international actors in circumstances where the aspirations of the local community may be shaped by political and cultural marginality, unique historical legacies and challenging legal issues.

The Kelabit community

As this book discusses the development of a *community* museum, it is therefore necessary to discuss the definition of 'the Kelabit community'. Since 1963 when the international borders of Malaysia were fixed on an ordinance map, the traditional homelands of the Kelabit people have straddled the Malaysian and Indonesian border of north central Borneo. In 2011 there were approximately 6000 Kelabits, which meant they were amongst the least populous of the indigenous tribes of Malaysia. Kelabit people predominately live in the town of Bario, in the Kelabit Highlands, where the museum is located, and in Miri, the oil rich coastal city at the mouth of the Baram River in Sarawak's northeast. Beyond north Borneo, Kelabit people are dispersed, with some people residing in Kuching, the capital city of Sarawak to the northwest, and others in Kuala Lumpur, the capital city of Malaysia.

Famously, Benedict Anderson used the concept of 'imagined communities' to help account for the political and social construction of national identities in Southeast Asia, and David Lowenthal has shown that throughout history communities have selectively interpreted the events of the past to establish their own valedictory myths, which have been used in heritage-making processes that assist with defining their identity.[15] These views are critical for understanding the ways in which communities seek to define their own heritage values to build a cohesive community. Communities may also be defined by external powers; the categorisation of indigenous peoples in Borneo was introduced in a colonial system and subsequently retained by the Malaysian constitution. The Kelabit are therefore officially recognised as an indigenous tribe, and their ethnicity and indigenousness are distinguished in Malaysian law. As S. Robert Aiken and Colin H Leigh have observed of all indigenous peoples of Malaysia, this designation results in few benefits and little agency in decision-making processes: 'although they are officially regarded as *bumiputera* [a term used to describe Malays and indigenous people, but excluding others], the reality is that they exercise little or no influence over policy decisions that affect their lands and livelihood'.[16] Effectively, this law preserves the idea of ethnic exclusion (or otherness) from a concept of Malaysian identity, which is principally based in the expression of Malay Muslim values.

In Malaysian law the Kelabit are a designated indigenous tribe in part because they have a distinct language that distinguishes them from other native tribes. However, in considering heritage-making in this context, there is a need to be clear that the traditional cultural practices of the Kelabit were significantly impacted by historical circumstances of the twentieth century. This has implications for the ways in which the Kelabit have sought to maintain a unified sense of community, and in turn has influenced the prioritisation or privileging of aspects of their cultural heritage and the process of shaping the museum concept and its programs.

Since WWII two dominant ideas – Christianity and western epistemology – have coalesced in the renegotiation of Kelabit heritage values and the representation of culture, and these have been critical to the maintenance of a sense of community. In the decades after WWII, native tribes in the Baram started to come under the influence of a range of Christian missionaries, including the Borneo Evangelical Mission, and later they participated in the Spiritual Revivals of the 1970s. The Kelabit felt the impact of Christianity profoundly because of their relatively small population, and there was a renegotiation of beliefs that ruptured the continuities with the past and saw traditional pagan rituals abandoned in favour of Christian litany. Small churches sprung up in the Kelabit Highlands, and these white buildings are still very prominent in the landscape. Anthropologist Matthew Amster studied another aspect of the impact of Christian missionaries and observed that the Christian emphasis on education profoundly assisted the mobility of members of the community from remote longhouses to urban areas.[17] This change enabled Kelabit children to engage with schools and universities, but also compromised the continuity this generation had with the world of their ancestors.

Between 1946 and 1960, when Sarawak was administered as a fully fledged British colony, the apparent threat to the conservation of traditional cultural heritage values and to the fabric of the community from this religious shift did not go unnoticed. For Malcolm Macdonald, the Governor-General of Malaya and British Borneo during 1947 and 1948, the uncompromising activities of some missionaries and the implications of their actions for the preservation of indigenous values were of great concern. Macdonald wrote reasonably favourably about the activities of the Catholic Missionary Father Henry Jansen, who established Saint Joseph's Secondary School in Miri in 1932, but was less enthusiastic about the Australian evangelical leader Hudson Southwell, who was active in Borneo from 1928. In his memoir of his time in Borneo, Macdonald wrote, 'The Evangelicals seemed to be embarked in a militant crusade against heathenism. . . . I did not feel much sympathy with that type of proselytism, especially as I suspected that with it went a forbidding intolerance of innocent native customs'. In conclusion he wrote, 'we must encourage them to preserve all that is good in their indigenous culture'; an idea that resonated with some members of the Kelabit community in later years.[18]

In understanding the reasons why Christianity is now a cornerstone of the Kelabit community, we were informed by the work of the anthropologist and sociologist Dr Poline Bala. As a Kelabit woman and academic, Bala has argued that between the 1950s and 1970s her ancestors, family and community were able to free themselves from the tyranny of evil spirits through embracing Christianity.[19] In her auto-ethnographic work she also identified some close parallel values in traditional culture and Christianity, which she has argued helps to explain the apparent ease and speed with which people underwent conversion. This coalescence of values and attitudes helped the transformation of the belief system from an indigenous pagan focus into a concept of modernity, in which the Kelabit people demonstrated a hybrid identity closely bound up with being indigenous, Christian and progressively modern.

In 1994 the Kelabit community registered their own non-governmental organisation under the *Societies Act, 1966*. The organisation is called the

Rurum Kelabit Sarawak (RKS). Through this action the Kelabit asserted that they had a strong sense of their own distinguishing history, language and culture – and their identity – by establishing an official means for asserting and defending their values. In a recent official RKS publication, the organisation was described thus:

> It is a non-political entity that operates and conducts its business and activities as a non-governmental organisation. RKS endeavours to achieve and carry out the objectives of the Association such as economics, social, sports, education, culture and arts and welfare of its members and the community as a whole. . . . The RKS is continuously embarking on ground-breaking initiatives that will propel the Highlands and its people towards a brighter and sustainable future.[20]

As culture in Malaysia is bound up with national government policy and programs, the RKS is nevertheless an unofficial de facto political organisation, in that it provides a means for the Kelabit to present a unified front in cultural political processes. The elected committee of the RKS includes volunteer women and men who have been successful within mainstream Malaysian society. Members of the committee at any one time might include politicians, senior civil servants, academics, teachers, medical practitioners, lawyers, and businessmen and women, who have some experience in negotiating the political and economic landscapes of Sarawak and Malaysia. The museum development project was an initiative of the RKS, and it was conceived with a sense of urgency because the population of the community is steadily declining, and with this decline the conservation of the community's cultural heritage is perceived by them to be at high risk.

The RKS is a cultural organisation that is distinct from the official system of local governance. In the town of Bario, the Council of Headmen includes representatives from each of the seven longhouses in the valley, and is led by a salaried Chief (*penghulu*), who is appointed by the Sarawak government. The system of appointment has in part been retained from the colonial period before 1963, and it in turn reflects the indigenous practice of discussing and electing a leader through a show of hands. As Sabihah Osman has explained, in contemporary Malaysia the appointment of longhouse headmen mirrors an idea of democracy as a form of *musyawarah*, which he defines 'as consensus in decision making', a long-held feature of indigenous political practice.[21] However, Osman also argues that in contemporary practice it may mean that the *penghulu* is likely to have forged an alliance with a state political party to secure his appointment to the office. While this may bring some benefits to the community, it has also been seen by the Asia Indigenous People Pact (AIPP) as a means of compromising its independence and agency. Thus, on the one hand while there is some continuity of indigenous political values embedded in the system, the method has been criticised by the AIPP, who in 2007 argued that the already meagre local village decision-making process appeared to be susceptible to external political interference.[22]

This is important because in understanding the definition of community it is necessary to understand how the Malaysian political system does not effectively incorporate ethnic and religious diversity. While the most powerful ethnic and religious alliance is that of Malay and Islam, the least is that of indigenous and Christian. 'In short', concluded S. Robert Aiken and Colin H Leigh, 'a major factor behind the continuing dispassion and marginalisation of Malaysia's non-Malay indigenous minorities is their lack of power vis-à-vis the dominant Malay majority'.[23] Nevertheless, the Kelabit have organised themselves in the establishment of the RKS as a self-funded non-government organisation that provides a mechanism through which the community can advocate for their cultural interests. As well, individual members of RKS have taken roles within the political system. For example, John Tarawe, a Bario-based businessman and advocate for the development of ecotourism programs in the Kelabit Highlands, was instrumental in the community consultation phase of the project and at that time was an elected member of the Baram District Council; and the President of the RKS at the commencement of the project was Datuk Garawat Gala, a lawyer by profession who has also acted as the Deputy Speaker of the Sarawak State Legislative Assembly.

With the benefits of high levels of education, individual members of the community have been able to negotiate some patronage for the conservation of their culture, and in some instances to derive direct economic advantage for the community from state and/or national governments.[24] At the national level, Datuk Idris Jala, who was Chief Executive of Malaysian Airlines (2005–2009), was appointed a Senator in the Malaysian national government by the Prime Minister Datuk Nazib Tun Razak in 2009, whose party was a member of the ruling Barisan Nasional (BN) coalition. In his role as a Senator between 2009 and 2015, Datuk Idris Jala was apparently instrumental in securing financial assistance to support the development of the Kelabit Highlands Community Museum building.

The promotion of Kelabit interests has meant maintaining a range of relationships with the dominant political alliance in Malaysia and Sarawak. Miri-based academic Arnold Puyok has observed that the majority of Kelabit people, especially of the older generation, have traditionally supported the Barisan Nasional (BN) coalition, which in Sarawak was led by Abdul Taib Mahmud, the long-serving Chief Minister of Sarawak from 1981 to 2014. Puyok has argued that the dominance of the BN in the national and state governments of Malaysia since independence has meant that it can persuasively and profitably assert that it alone has the capability and resources to foster economic and social development in rural areas such as Bario. He has written that the BN was able to maintain 'a high level of political supremacy over most constituencies [in Sarawak] due to its successful manipulation of the politics of development'.[25]

Seen from an historical perspective, the Kelabit community has certainly aspired to better health care and greater prosperity to enhance the sustainability of the longhouses of the Highlands. The achievements of individuals in assisting in the delivery of these objectives should not be underestimated, but equally it would be unfair to assume that these advances have substantially assisted resolving indigenous land rights or effecting meaningful agency in the recognition and management of cultural landscapes. The longstanding and entwined issues of land ownership, and the relationships that indigenous people have with forest resources, is another defining aspect of modern Kelabit identity, and has galvanised community activism. This is not because the community is opposed to the concept of development but more so, as S. Robert Aiken and Colin H Leigh concluded, because they have disliked 'the negative effects of the unsolicited "development initiatives" that have been foisted on them'.[26] As they have concluded from a legal perspective:

> Far from being passive 'victims of development' [indigenous people] have, for example, engaged government officials in various forms of confrontation, negotiation or collaboration over development schemes, formed NGOs to represent their interests [such as the RKS], organised media campaigns to highlight their grievances, and engaged in various forms of both passive and active resistance.[27]

Despite their efforts, however, in recent years, while the issue of native land rights has further galvanised the Kelabit community, arguments and claims for ownership of traditional lands have largely been dismissed by governments, and, as Aiken and Leigh have asserted, this is because indigenous communities have very little political influence. As a result, attempts to resolve particular disputes through legal processes have given rise to the need for communities to document and articulate their historical, cultural and spiritual occupation of lands and thus to define the cultural landscape in which they have resided more formally than they may have done previously. The legal, economic and social ramifications of these issues have required the Kelabit leadership to focus more effectively on the relationships between cultural heritage and the representation of their identity and to seek to create a very clear symbol of their claim for their agency and authority.

Chapter outlines

The development phase of the project to establish a museum and cultural centre occurred between 2011 and 2016 and is referred to as the Kelabit Highlands Community Museum Development Project (KHCMDP). In August 2016, the community achieved the key aim of the project with the building of a museum and cultural centre; and it was officially opened during the 11th Bario Nukenan (Food) Festival.[28] During the six years from conception to completion, the museum development project moved at a considerable pace, reflecting the sense of urgency that the community felt about the conservation of its heritage.

As a case study, this account of the project is nested within the discourse of museology or museum studies, in which researchers are interested in the histories, theories and practices of museum operations. More precisely this book belongs to ideas that have evolved from the 'new museology'.[29] In this discourse, museum and heritage processes are linked to social development agendas, particularly concerning the connection between community agency and the social dividends of cultural projects. Furthermore, this account is also informed by discussions and research in Asia, where under the auspices of organisations including the United Nations Education Science Culture Organization (UNESCO), the International Centre for the Study of the Preservation and Restoration of Cultural Property (ICCROM), the International Council of Museums (ICOM) and the Association of Southeast Asian Nations (ASEAN), various programs have been piloted in the last two decades that were designed to foster greater local community participation in the conservation of cultural heritage. In our engagement with these discourses we are focused on exploring the dynamics of cultural heritage conservation and representation in circumstances in which a marginalised community is charged with safeguarding their own culture – arts, language, practices and cultural and natural heritage values – within a challenging historical, political and cultural framework.

Despite claims that museums and conservation practice are essentially euro-centric forms of hegemony, the Kelabit people of northwest Borneo were interested in establishing their own museum and cultural centre, thus adding a significant contribution to the discourse of the role of local communities in managing the conservation of their own cultural heritage. Further, in discussing the processes through which the project has been conducted, this book offers some understanding of the many complexities influencing and shaping cultural heritage conservation in Malaysia and more generally in the Asia Pacific region.

The Kelabit's attraction to the idea of creating their own museum lies in the historical eminence of museums in Malaysia, where they have functioned for well over a hundred years. *Chapter Two: Shaping Kelabit conservation processes in Southeast Asia*, will present an historical introduction that explains how museums became a part of cultural life in Sarawak and Malaysia. Chapter Two will outline historical endeavours to represent Kelabit identity, and in particular, the most influential point of reference is the Sarawak Museum, located in Kuching, Sarawak (northwest Borneo, East Malaysia). It opened in 1891 and has functioned almost continuously since then. Its function is to represent the cultural and natural heritage of the island of Borneo, and its collections include many items that are associated with the history and culture of the Kelabit people.

The presence of these museums is a legacy of British Imperial and epistemological ambitions in Southeast Asia. However, their expansion is also the result of the policies and actions of the Government of Malaysia since 1963 and the post-colonial nation building processes it has instigated. These policies and actions align museums with national social development, have preserved colonial museum buildings and collections, and supported the creation of new museums. As such the political process in which culture is located have legitimised the idea that museums have an important political and social role to play as instruments for the dissemination of knowledge and ideas of identity. It is clear that in Malaysia the government has seen the display of cultural material in museums as a strategic way of codifying and standardising the representation of the ethnic complexity of the nation; and further, that these representations have been aligned and integrated with other economic development activities such as cultural tourism.

The dynamic relationships between museums and cultural representations are a central theme of this book and will be discussed in depth in *Chapter Three: History, knowledge and the representation of identity*. This study recognises the centrality of the Malaysian national government in the process, but the discussion foregrounds the lesser understood process of how communities achieve agency in heritage conservation and representation in circumstances where they are comparatively resource poor actors who reside outside the State museum system. The emphasis on the role of community agency in the processes of cultural heritage conservation and management in Southeast Asia is significant to the politics of development not least because it illuminates how the contrasting aspirations of community members and the State are being negotiated. This may benefit other communities in the region who are also pursuing strategies to advance the conservation of their own threatened identity and culture. The development of Kelabit Highlands Community Museum and Cultural Centre is significant for a number of other reasons. This book identifies and interprets a range of local factors that drove the cultural development process in the state of Sarawak, and contributes a unique and original perspective to the discourse concerning the roles of conservation and museology in the Asia Pacific region.

Chapter Four: Museum development and tourism; identifying authenticity and representation will discuss how the Kelabit community museum seeks to be a representation of their identity engineered through community participation, with programs informing the preservation, articulation and presentation of information derived from all possible sources. In Sarawak, this kind of strategic cultural thinking by an indigenous community is a relatively recent occurrence. Not only is authentic representation a motivating factor in this project, cultural tourism is also seen as one of the key drivers of the project, leading to a challenging relationship between the role of the museum in cultural and economic development and maintaining authenticity in the representation of values and identity. Chapter Four will interrogate this fragile relationship where one concern greatly impacts the other.

The longstanding but changing relationship between the community and their homelands is a substantial issue that has shaped the discussion of the conservation of cultural and natural heritage. *Chapter Five: Indigenous knowledge in community museum practice* will present how the Kelabit are recognised in law as one of the indigenous groups of Malaysia and their traditional longhouses are located in the Highlands of northeast Sarawak. These are clustered around the village of Bario high up in the mountains of the administrative Fourth Division, which includes the Baram river system. For as long as there has been community memory, the Kelabit homelands have encompassed the landmark twin-mountains known as *Batu Lawi*, which are of high cultural significance, and their lands and longhouse communities have straddled the East Malaysian border into Kalimantan, Indonesia. In traditional society, the connections with the land were infused with spirituality, and this was represented in the adornment of their bodies with animal skins, bones and the feathers of the sacred hornbill. Like many other indigenous people of Borneo, the Kelabit lived communally in longhouses, and in Bario some still do, where they are rice farmers and hunters, teachers and students, professionals and tourist hosts.

Evelyne Hong observed in 1987 that when faced with the impacts of the State sanctioned exploitation of forests, 'the native peoples of Sarawak have been unable to adequately articulate their problems or seek proper redress for the immense tribulation and misery being inflicted upon them'.[30] Conflict over the logging of forests and the preservation of tribal lands eventually resulted in a series of interventionist actions, which were dealt with harshly by the State and the companies involved in forestry. Some years later, perhaps due to the experience of those events, a generation of Kelabit leaders, who are now equipped with professional skills and economic support, are seeking to argue for and develop their own agency and aspirations in the conservation of their cultural heritage.

The Kelabit were most profoundly impacted by colonial encounters in the twentieth century. This led to significant spiritual and cultural changes, especially through their conversion to Christianity and engagement with western education. The Kelabits can be distinguished from mainstream Malaysian society in three very important ways, and these are critical foundations for understanding why this project was conceived and pursued by the community. In the first place, the Kelabit are distinguished by their ethnicity as defined by their designation as an official native tribe; secondly, they are distinguished geographically, due to the remote location of their homelands (which had historical significance as well as continues to have implications for contemporary tourism), and thirdly, and most critically, they are religiously marginalised, as they are a predominately Christian minority in a country in which the official religion is Islam. In Sarawak, the Malays are extensively Muslims. This book therefore provides an account of a community action that has galvanised the Kelabit people, and the process undertaken will be presented in *Chapter Six: Shaping the discussion of conservation*. Chapter Six explores the ramifications of Kelabit encounters with modernity and other factors that have shaped the motivations for establishing their own museum and cultural centre.

Most important perhaps is the question of leadership and organisation, and the extent to which the Kelabit have been strategic in seeking to promote their aims within the modern Malaysian political system. In this museum development the most influential organisation is the Rurum Kelabit Sarawak (RKS). It formally represents and promotes the interests of the Kelabit people. The RKS led the museum development process, which had its genesis in addressing the community's desire to retard the further dilution of their own cultural values, illustrated by the almost complete loss of their own language, and the desperate need to achieve effective agency in the conservation and representation of their heritage and culture. In providing an account of the project, this book contextualises the actions of the leadership of the RKS, the involvement of other community members and the participation of other actors. More specifically, *Chapter Seven: The development of the Kelabit Highlands Community Museum Project* looks in detail at the theory and methodology applied to this cross-cultural development program and undertaken in partnership between the community and foreign/external actors, including the staff members of Deakin University, Australia (the DU team). From the onset, there was a clear definition of roles and expectations driven by a strong leadership team and a proactive community. The remoteness of the location, and the need to travel to collaborate, presented some unforeseen challenges, and these will be discussed in Chapter Seven.

Chapter Eight: Detailed encounters will present, in a chronological format, each of the engagements between academics, students and the community throughout the project from 2011 to 2016. The information presented has been constructed from various sources of documentation and is deliberately presented as a narrative to offer a way of addressing the complexity of the project. The DU team were in a privileged position to hear stories, document information and support the community as they navigated their way through some complex issues, including the construction of knowledge into a structural format and defining the content that constituted a Kelabit identity. There were a number of ways this could be explored, and as each of these were examined, new content emerged.

Both positive and negative positions can be presented when examining this project. There is recognition that the project will continue to evolve according to the community's aims and aspirations, yet the progress made and the resources the DU team were able to provide during the project have established a solid foundation upon which to build a sustainable exemplar of community museums. The final chapter, *Concluding remarks*, outlines both the constructive and unconstructive results from the project, noting the affirmative position is the dominant outcome. The Kelabit Highlands Community Museum building has been completed and the representation of this progressive, hybrid community will continue for some time.

Notes

1 See, Brian Graham and Peter Howard (eds), *The Ashgate Research Companion to Heritage and Identity*, Ashgate, Hampshire, 2008. And, Patrick Daly and Tim Winter (eds), *Routledge Handbook of Heritage in Asia*, Routledge, Abingdon, 2012.
2 The International Centre for the Study of the Preservation of Cultural Property (ICCROM) has been instrumental in researching in this area. See, Herb Stovel and Nicholas Stanley-Price (eds), *Conservation of Living Religious Heritage: Papers from the ICCROM 2003 Forum on Living Religious Heritage: Conserving the Sacred*, ICCROM, Rome, 2005. See also, Helaine Silverman and D. Fairchild Ruggles, *Cultural Heritage and Human Rights*, Spinger, New York, 2007. And, William Logan, 'Cultural Diversity, Cultural Heritage and Human Rights: Towards Heritage Management as Human Rights-Based Cultural Practice', *International Journal of Heritage Studies*, Vol.18, No.3, 2012, pp. 231–244.
3 Patrick Daly and Tim Winter (eds), *Routledge Handbook of Heritage in Asia*, Routledge, Abingdon, 2012.
4 See, Colin Long and Jonathan Sweet, 'Globalization, Nationalism and World Heritage: Interpreting Luang Prabang', *South East Asia Research*, Vol.14, No.3, 2006, pp. 445–469. And, Jonathan Sweet and Fengqi Qian, 'History, Heritage, and the Representation of Ethnic Diversity: Cultural Tourism in China', in, James B. Gardener and Paula Hamilton (eds), *The Oxford Handbook of Public History*, Oxford University Press, Oxford, 2017, pp. 292–308.
5 Denis Byrne, 'Chartering Heritage in Asia's Postmodern World', *Newsletter, The Getty Conservation Institute*, Vol.19, No.2, Summer 2004, www.getty.edu/

conservation/publications_resources/newsletters/19_2/news_in_cons1.html, accessed 2 November 2017.
6 See, Evelyne Hong, *Natives of Sarawak, Survival in Borneo's Vanishing Forests*, Institut Masyarakat, Malaysia, 1987.
7 UNESCO, *Our Creative Diversity: Report of the World Commission on Culture and Development*, UNESCO, Paris, 1995, unesdoc.unesco.org/images/0010/001016/101651e.pdf, accessed 2 November 2017.
8 See for example, Martin Mowforth and Ian Munt, *Tourism and Sustainability, Development, Globalisations and New Tourism in the Third World*, Fourth Edition, Routledge, Abingdon, 2016.
9 Sarah Lynne Hitchner, *Remaking the Landscape: Kelabit Engagements with Conservation and Development in Sarawak, Malaysia*, A Dissertation Submitted to the Graduate Faculty of The University of Georgia in Partial Fulfilment of the Requirements for the Degree, Doctor of Philosophy, Athens, Georgia, 2009, p. 42.
10 Tan Tai Yong, 'The "Grand Design": British Policy, Local Politics, and the Making of Malaysia, 1955–1961', in Marc Frey, Ronald W. Pruessen and Tan Tai Yong (eds), *The Transformation of Southeast Asia, International Perspectives on Decolonization*, Singapore University Press, Singapore, 2004, pp. 142–160, p. 142.
11 Ibid, 2004, p. 149.
12 Abu Talib Ahamad, *Museums, History and Culture in Malaysia*, NUS Press, Singapore, 2015, p. 4.
13 Ibid, 2015, p. 5.
14 Deakin University Human Ethics approval for the project HAE-13–114 Kelabit Highland Community Museum Development Project was granted 26 November 2013.
15 Benedict Anderson, *Imagined Communities: Reflections on the Origin and Spread of Nationalism*, Verso, London, 2006 and David Lowenthal, *The Heritage Crusade and the Spoils of History*, Cambridge University Press, Cambridge, 1998.
16 S. Robert Aiken and Colin H. Leigh, 'Seeking Redress in the Courts: Indigenous Land Rights and Judicial Decisions in Malaysia', *Modern Asian Studies*, Vol.45, No.4, July 2010, pp. 825–875, pp. 871–872.
17 Matthew H. Amster, 'Portable Potency: Christianity, Mobility and Spiritual Landscapes Among the Kelabit', *Anthropological Forum: A Journal of Social Anthropology and Comparative Sociology*, Vol.13, No.3, 2009, pp. 307–322, p. 308.
18 Malcolm MacDonald, *Borneo People*, Jonathan Cape, London, 1956, p. 273.
19 Poline Bala, 'An Engagement with "Modernity", Becoming Christian in the Kelabit Highlands of Central Borneo', *Borneo Research Bulletin*, Vol.40, 2009, pp. 173–185, p. 176.
20 Nikki Lugun (ed), *Pesta Nukenen. Celebrating the Cultural and Culinary Heritage of the Kelabit Highlands*, Rurum Kelabit Sarawak, Kuching, 2015, p. 43.
21 Sabihah Osman, 'Globalization and Democratization: The Response of the Indigenous People of Sarawak', *Third World Quarterly*, Vol.21. No.6, Capturing Globalization, December 2000, pp. 977–988, p. 979.
22 'Submission by the Asia Indigenous Peoples Pact (AIPP) Foundation to the study by the Expert Mechanism of the Rights of Indigenous Peoples entitled "Indigenous Peoples and Right to Participate in Decision-Making"', *Indigenous Governance Systems in Asia*, 2007, p. 5, http://www2.ohchr.org/english/issues/indigenous/ExpertMechanism/3rd/docs/contributions/AIPP_2.pdf, accessed 18 July 2017.

23 S. Robert Aiken and Colin H. Leigh, 'Seeking Redress in the Courts: Indigenous Land Rights and Judicial Decisions in Malaysia', *Modern Asian Studies*, Vol.45, No.4, July 2010, pp. 825–875, pp. 871–872.
24 Cecilia Sman, 'Teripun a Reminder of Kelabits' Roots', *Borneo Post Online*, 14 August 2016, www.theborneopost.com/2016/08/14/teripun-a-reminder-of-kelabits-roots/, accessed 18 July 2017.
25 Arnold Puyok, 'The 2004 Ba'Kelalan By-Èlection in Sarawak, East Malaysia: The Lun Bawang Factor and Whither Representative Democracy in Malaysia', *Contemporary Southeast Asia*, Vol.27, No.1, April 2005, pp. 64–79, p. 76.
26 S. Robert Aiken and Colin H. Leigh, 'Seeking Redress in the Courts: Indigenous Land Rights and Judicial Decisions in Malaysia', *Modern Asian Studies*, Vol.45, No.4, July 2010, pp. 825–875, p. 842.
27 Ibid, 2010, p. 842.
28 Cecilia Sman, 'Teripun a Reminder of Kelabits' Roots', *Borneo Post Online*, 14 August 2016, www.theborneopost.com/2016/08/14/teripun-a-reminder-of-kelabits-roots/, accessed 18 July 2017.
29 Peter Vergo (ed), *The New Museology*, Reaktion Books, London, 1989.
30 Evelyne Hong, *Natives of Sarawak, Survival in Borneo's Vanishing Forests*, Institut Masyarakat, Malaysia, 1987, p. 5.

2 Shaping Kelabit conservation processes in Southeast Asia

Introduction

As the KHCMDP unfolded, it became apparent that the efforts of the Kelabit community to develop their own inclusive conservation process reflected the influence of the historical and intellectual context in which they were participants. The interest expressed by the members of the Rurum Kelabit Sarawak (RKS) in establishing a community museum showed their familiarity and understanding of western-style museums, confirming a high regard for the role of museums in contemporary society. The current awareness and engagement with museums has its foundation in the history of museums by European governments in South and Southeast Asia in the nineteenth century, when they were important instruments of colonial rule. During the process of decolonisation in Malaysia after WWII, these 'colonial museums' were consumed into a new national museum system. In this project, however, the RKS worked independently from the state, and were focused on exploring museology as a way to meet their own conservation needs and representational aspirations.

The role of museums in the representation of identities is a key subject in the critical historical analysis of museums. This discourse has been influenced by the seminal discussions in the book *Exhibiting Cultures, The Poetics and Politics of Museum Display*, published in 1991.[1] The investigation into the nuances of representation in colonial museums has grown since then, and studies have interpreted the relationships between Imperial design ambitions and local circumstances across the region. In 2007, for example, Paul Walker published a comparative analysis of the architecture and operations of the Napier Museum in Trivandrum, India, and the Canterbury Museum in Christchurch, New Zealand.[2] In addition, the ethnographic representation of indigenous peoples through exhibition design using photographs, artefacts and audio-visual material has been most contentious. The foregrounding, by James Clifford and others, questioned the extent to which the representation of indigenous people has reflected a Eurocentric conceptualisation of humanity – regarded at best as poorly contextualised, or at worst as intentionally racist – and also raised questions about the extent to which indigenous peoples have or have not had influence or control in this process.

The critical historical evaluation of the museum programs has also been undertaken and supported by members of the International Council of Museums (ICOM). There has been evidence in some very tangible activities, including the development of international professional networks, which have subsequently added strength to the attempts by indigenous people and some nation states to address the ways in which museum displays are developed and used to represent ethnic or religious minorities. The Malaysian Branch of the ICOM was established in 1976 and the Director of the Sarawak Museum attended its meetings regularly and served on the executive board.[3] In this chapter, therefore, two important streams of influence are introduced because they have underpinned the interest and reasoning of the RKS's approach to this museum project.

The first section of this chapter provides an historical introduction that explains how museums became a part of cultural life in Sarawak and Malaysia, and as such, were already recognised as an established method of conservation and representation with potential for adaptations to promote Kelabit values. The specific personalities and events that shaped an interest in museology are particularly significant because history shows the profound influence of British (rather than Malay and Islam) museum actors, and thus in part it helps to explain the intellectual approach that underpinned the conceptualisation of this project. The second part of the chapter discusses more recent developments in regional approaches to museology and heritage conservation. It provides an example of how ideas of indigenous agency and community participation have been disseminated by UNESCO, ICOM and ICCROM (The International Centre for the Study of the Preservation and Restoration of Cultural Property) in the last twenty years, and considers their influence in shaping conservation processes in Southeast Asia; the increasing emphasis on community-based people-centred approaches to conservation may be in contrast to the exclusionary attitudes and policies of some national governments.

The Sarawak Museum – the colonial museum

Museums were an integral aspect of European colonial ambitions in South and Southeast Asia from the seventeenth century. In the Philippines, the University of Santo Tomas was established under the Portuguese and began collecting natural history and ethnographic material in the 1680s, with a more formalised museum emerging after 1871.[4] The Museum National in Jakarta was established by the Dutch Batavian Society for Arts and Sciences in 1778, and a purpose-built neo-classical museum building was completed in 1867.[5] The history of museums in neighbouring Malaysia, however, was inextricably linked to the British colonial enterprise and mirrored the dissemination of the British model of government funded public museums in India and Ceylon, as well as Australia and New Zealand. These so-called 'colonial museums' were established during the nineteenth century and became integral nodes in a global scientific network in which discoveries made in the colonies were shared around the Empire. Museum buildings were conceived to showcase the resources and distinctive curiosities of the place. At the beginning of the twentieth century, museums were functioning in Kuching, Singapore, Colombo (Ceylon), Madras (now Chennai) and Calcutta (now Kolkata) and many other places. They were managed by government appointed professional curators who undertook historical and archaeological research, collected and exchanged natural history specimens and wrote scientific papers that trumpeted their discoveries and achievements. It is important to note that while these museums had a strong Imperial role, indigenous actors were not always excluded; as Cherie McKeich has shown, at the Indian Museum in Calcutta, curatorial responsibilities were not strictly the preserve of the British, and in the 1880s the Bengali T. N. Mukhaji was a very significant contributor and a central participant in the representation of India at international exhibitions.[6] While curators such as Mukhaji developed extensive cultural and scientific collections, the organisations themselves were mostly poorly resourced and efforts to preserve natural history specimens were challenged by destructive environmental conditions. Nevertheless, educational displays were constructed in the galleries, in which curators judiciously organised their collections of zoological specimens and other items according to the most current European classification and taxonomic systems.[7] For example, the Raffles Museum in Singapore, John MacKenzie has argued, closely adhered to the organisation and construction of knowledge along Imperial and scientific lines.[8]

In Malaysia those museums that have survived since the nineteenth century belong to an elite group that were established across South and Southeast Asia. The oldest continuously functioning museum on the Malay Peninsula is the Perak State Museum. It was founded in 1883 and expanded with gallery extensions between 1890 and 1903. It was part of a local network that included the Raffles Museum in Singapore, which occupied a purpose-built building after 1887, and the Selangor Museum, which was established in Kuala Lumpur in 1898 (but destroyed during WWII). In Sarawak, the state government-administered Sarawak Museum in Kuching is the oldest museum in Borneo (this includes the Dutch controlled south of the island that was part of the Netherlands East Indies, and became the Indonesian state of Kalimantan). It was created and developed as a scientific civic resource by successive members of the Brooke family, a colonial dynasty that ruled the province for three generations between 1840 and 1940, mostly operating as a British protectorate. The Sarawak Museum was initially conceived by the first Raja of Sarawak, James Brooke, at the urging of scientist Alfred Russell Wallace, who visited Borneo in mid-1854 'to collect *orang utan* and other exotic specimens for European museums'.[9] The second Rajah, Charles Brooke, the nephew of James Brooke, developed the museum concept and completed the handsome 'old' (as it is known today) building in 1891–1892, which was built on a hill overlooking the centre of the riverside town. The Sarawak Museum has operated continuously since its inception, except for a few years during WWII, when it was mothballed (and preserved) during the Japanese occupation of Kuching.

Unlike some of the personnel at the Indian Museum in Calcutta, the curators who worked at the Sarawak Museum were western educated scholars and civil servants and, as Gary Maitland reported, between 1890 and 1940 seven of eight director/curators were educated at the Universities of Oxford or Cambridge.[10] These curators were imbued with an Imperial mindset and were charged with 'classifying the natural and cultural material of the world', and in pursuing this ambition they moved around the Empire. After four years working in Kuching, for example, zoologist John Hewitt pursued appointments in southern Africa and in 1910 became the Director of the Albany Museum, Eastern Cape.[11] These curators aspired to be as comprehensive as possible in their collecting activities and methodical in the presentation of their research. They applied their training in contemporary anthropological, archaeological or zoological methods and presented exotic displays of material – artefacts and human anatomy – following taxonomical schemes that were being disseminated from the United Kingdom and other European scientific centres.[12] The Sarawak Museum collection includes cultural artefacts and natural history specimens that may have been obtained by agents working in the interior, with the assistance of indigenous individuals, or through other methods that may now be illegal or considered to be unethical by the contemporary museum profession.[13] Nevertheless, the development of these collections reflected the Brookes' interest in resourcing the Sarawak Museum to provide a comprehensive representation of the history, wealth and resources of the colony. In the 1920s, John Molton, who had been a curator at the Sarawak Museum for a decade, moved to the Raffles Museum, where he continued this tradition and undertook the reorganisation of the collections to place more emphasis on the immediate region.[14]

The relationship between Sarawak and Singapore had become increasingly important by the mid-nineteenth century as Sarawak grew as a trading colony. The growth of Kuching was characterised by increasing ethnic diversity that included indigenous tribes, European and Chinese business people and Malay coastal villagers. Thus, the administration of Sarawak included pacifying and managing a growing population. The Kelabit people, however, remained largely outside the Rajas' direct control, due to their remote location in the far southeast of the colony. The Kelabit were also isolated linguistically because they did not share a language with the Iban people, who were the largest tribe in the west of Sarawak and who had regular contact with and served in the Brookes' administration. It is therefore very unlikely that any Kelabit people had much, if any, direct knowledge of the Sarawak Museum during the Brookes' administration. However, in the years after WWII when Sarawak was an official British Colony, members of the community attained greater mobility and more formal western education, and their understanding of museology grew dramatically. This occurred largely through the influence of one man – Tom Harrisson, who in 1937 had been a founding member of the British social research group *Mass Observation*.

A biography written by Judith M. Heiman provides a very comprehensive view of Harrisson's life and work; including the years he spent in Sarawak, mostly between 1944 and 1966.[15] He had a deep engagement with Borneo in various capacities – as an explorer and collector in the 1930s; as a British Army combat guerrilla in the 1940s; and, as an archaeologist and anthropologist in the 1950s and 1960s. In 1932, he had participated in an Oxford University expedition in Sarawak, which undertook an extensive collecting mission led by the then Curator of the Sarawak Museum, Edward Banks.[16] This experience in Sarawak, which included contact with indigenous peoples and negotiating the challenging geography of the interior, led to his recruitment into the British Army when in WWII the Japanese occupied Borneo. In 1944 and 1945 he had the rank of Major and commanded the British and Australian Z Force commandos, who served in Operation SEMUT. After parachuting into the remote Kelabit Highlands in 1944, they linked up with local people, and from their base in Bario they undertook jungle operations to harass the Japanese troops. The heritage significance of this has been discussed in the book *Battlefield Events. Landscape, Commemoration and Heritage*.[17]

After WWII, Harrisson was appointed to the post of Government Ethnologist and Museum Curator at the Sarawak Museum, where he worked between 1946 and 1961. His engagement with the Kelabit people continued, and he and his museum colleagues conducted archaeological and anthropological research in the Kelabit Highlands, and during this time the museum's collection of material from the region grew. His ability to work in the highlands was in no small way enabled by strong personal friendships that had been established with members of the Kelabit community through their shared wartime experiences. This relationship with the Kelabit community was documented by his wife Barbara Harrisson who, in 1977, wrote that 'he spent as many as four years in the village of Bario, spreading his sojourns over two decades'.[18] During this time: 'He observed the community as it grew from a few hundred persons in one longhouse to a clustered, border town with a busy airport, tourism, imported religions, educational, medical and military services, and cooperative industrial enterprise as well'.[19]

Anthropological research in Sarawak was predominately undertaken by western academics who, like Harrisson, drew attention to the impact that the profound changes in the social and spiritual circumstances of indigenous people were having on the conservation of heritages. Without a written language, records or archives, Kelabit values were vulnerable to loss, due to the disruption to orally transmitted cultural heritage caused by outside influences and the change which followed. Similarly, they also felt the pressure from modernity to embrace alternatives to traditional agricultural practices. In this context, in the early 1970s the American anthropologist Carol Rubenstein was sponsored by the Ford Foundation to document, collect and transcribe indigenous songs and stories in Sarawak. In her own words: 'I collected and translated songs and chants from the oral tradition of the Sarawak Dayaks'.[20] The documented poems were published in the *Sarawak Museum Journal* as a Special Monograph (No.2) in 1973: *Poems of Indigenous People of Sarawak: Some of the Songs and Chants*.[21] The transcription of oral sources contributed to the documentation of the Kelabit language in literary form and helped to define Kelabit written language. Researchers such as Rubenstein recognised the urgency of addressing the potential loss of some forms of indigenous knowledge, but her project is also an early example of indigenous people working very closely with a foreign researcher, an arrangement that has served the community well over recent years. It is therefore critical to the explanation of the museum development project to appreciate that the Kelabit's association with Harrisson facilitated a heritage awakening in which through absolute necessity the Kelabit began to incorporate a modern concept of heritage into their hybrid intellectual, spiritual and cultural cosmology.

There is in fact a very tangible link between the current members of the RKS and Harrisson: In the 1950s, Harrisson's personal commitment to education led to some Kelabit children being 'brought down' to Kuching to go to school, and also, in some cases, to work in the Sarawak Museum.[22] One of the young men who assisted at the museum was David Labang. In recent years, he and his wife, Lucy Bulan (a long-serving member of the RKS executive), were advisors and participants to the Kelabit Highlands Community Museum Development Project, building upon their strong commitment to the rediscovery and documentation of Kelabit customs over many years. In 1979, for example, their commitment to the documentation of intangible cultural heritage processes was demonstrated in an article they wrote explaining the Kelabit rice harvest for the *Sarawak Museum Journal*.[23]

These young Kelabit intellectuals experienced firsthand the relationship between museum collections and anthropology that had been maintained by Harrisson at the Sarawak Museum. In the galleries of the museum, the interpretation of the indigenous cultures of Borneo was primarily based on a material culture approach, and it provided very little contextual information. However, they also witnessed a change at the museum that directly enhanced indigenous agency in the representation of native cultures. In 1967 Harrisson was replaced as Director by Benedict Sandin, a young curator of Iban ethnicity, whom Harrisson had mentored, and who had also been sent to India to participate in the UNESCO Regional Seminar on Museology held in New Delhi in 1966. By 1968, Sandin's impact had been felt at the museum, and he reported in the foreword to the revised museum guidebook that 'the latest major addition' to the museum's displays was a reconstructed 'two-*bilik* Iban longhouse' that 'takes up the whole East Gallery of the first floor'.[24] This reconstruction attempted to contextualise collection material and was made of traditional materials and could be physically explored (it remains in situ). It included a set of human heads that hung from the rafters, together with ceramics and other objects. At the time, the second-floor interior walls of the old colonial museum building were decorated with colourful mural paintings using local designs and depicting scenes of the traditional life of the indigenous tribes of Sarawak. It can be concluded that to some extent at least this is a very early example in the post-colonial world of agency in the representation of indigenous cultures being passed to the natives themselves. While the Directorship of the Sarawak Museum is not reserved for an indigenous person, currently the museum director is also indigenous.

The Brookes' (the so-called White Rajas) fostered a very limited understanding of indigenous cultures of Sarawak through a quintessential colonial museum in which the local natives had little agency. Harrisson, though, demonstrated a level of empathy to the plight of indigenous people that was exceptional in the world of colonial museums at this time. In his dual role as Government Ethnologist and Museum Curator, he fostered a higher level of engagement with the Kelabit people and encouraged their participation in the museum's activities. He encouraged the professional development of the local curators who succeeded him, in particular Benedict Sandon and Lucas Chin, who authored the book *Cultural Heritage of Sarawak*, published in 1980.[25] Harrisson had maintained a very ambitious and serious research and film making agenda. This included reviving the *Sarawak Museum Journal* (SMJ), which, by the time he left Sarawak in the late 1960s, had become an internationally respected vehicle for documenting and reporting research on all things Bornean, and which, by the mid-1970s, also included contributions from local indigenous writers who drew attention to the significance of their cultural heritage.

Global framework, local issues

Whilst the current members of the RKS were aware of museums and the associated intellectual frameworks as adolescents, in the latter part of the twentieth century the specific attention given to the plight of indigenous peoples gave greater impetus to the Kelabit action to address their own heritage conservation in Sarawak. This reflected the work of UNESCO, which since the 1950s has been a principle actor in setting the expectations of the conservation of cultural heritage in South and Southeast Asia. In recent years, it has been recognised that in some circumstances in Asia the separation of heritage conservation initiatives and projects into protected demarcated zones such as 'museum' and 'heritage site', 'material' and 'spiritual' has become much less tenable, especially in circumstances where heritage material is distributed throughout the community and the realms of natural and cultural values are clearly enmeshed. There has been a recognition that in such cases the strict demarcation of material, intangible and natural values is often inadequate for describing the heritage values. As a result, the regional members of conservation agencies, including UNESCO, ICCROM and ICOM, have expanded their efforts to investigate and promote research into forms of heritage conservation that incorporate community initiatives and traditional conservation activities that are meaningful to local people and which may also support social and economic sustainability. This shift of focus onto the recognition of people-centred approaches to conservation recognised that traditional knowledge has a significant role to play in heritage conservation and further, that the purpose of heritage conservation should be integrated into community development processes. Proponents of this view have attempted to more broadly influence frameworks for the management of UNESCO World Heritage sites, which have tended to be cordoned off as the privileged domain of conservation professionals, and secondly, on developing capacity for the management of museums, collections and cultural representation by local people[26] – whose heritage it often is.

Over the past few decades the multi-lateral international agenda concerning the rights of indigenous peoples has enhanced confidence and indirectly supported heritage initiatives. A number of key United Nations (UN) resolutions – supported by Malaysia – have provided some encouragement. The *Declaration on the Rights of Indigenous Peoples*, 2007, provides in Article 5 a principle that asserts the right of indigenous people to pursue the preservation and development of distinct cultural institutions, whilst continuing to participate fully in the nation state.[27] The *Second International Decade of the World's Indigenous Peoples* (2005–2015) lent ongoing support for the promotion of effective indigenous participation in the decisions that directly or indirectly affect their lifestyles and the values of traditional lands and territories.[28] These have been supported on the ground to some extent by UNESCO operations in Asia, which have pursued initiatives in the documentation of local and indigenous knowledge systems, having implications for conservation and sustainable development.[29]

These global statements and local actions provided a platform for the KHCMDP and bolstered confidence in the rationale and the process, but equally gave rise to a number of questions concerning the circumstances that inhibit the effectiveness of indigenous people to address the conservation of their cultural heritage in Malaysia. The UNESCO offices that serve the region in Southeast Asia are located in Jakarta and Bangkok. The piloting of a participatory conservation framework by the Bangkok office (which reflected the global thinking of other agencies such as ICCROM) was philosophically influential for the development of the Kelabit museum development. This framework was the 2005 *Hoi An Protocols For Best Conservation Practice in Asia: Professional Guidelines For Assuring and Preserving the Authenticity of Heritage Sites in the Context of the Cultures of Asia* (Hoi An Protocol).[30] The Protocol was piloted in Vietnam and it represented the efforts of UNESCO to promote a people-centred approach to heritage conservation, which recognised the issue of the exclusion of local people from conservation processes, a factor broadly reflective of circumstances across the region. Thus, the Hoi An Protocol responded to the privileging of materialist approaches to conservation in conventional heritage practices and management, and argued strongly for the incorporation of participatory processes, through which local people could be meaningfully engaged in the determination and management of heritage and benefit socially, spiritually and economically from heritage conservation.

This idea was reflected more broadly in other cultural heritage discourses in Asia in the past 30 years, and questions the extent to which heritage conservation ought to be conducted as an objective global science rather than an intuitive process of localised intangible cultural and spiritual processes. Essentially it interrogates the location of authority in the relationship between external or western conservation processes and practices and local circumstances. It has been suggested by local conservation practitioners that local approaches to heritage assessments, significances and technical issues were more appropriate than those applied by external predominantly European conservation practitioners. In part, this concern has antecedents in the post-colonial Malaysian political heritage discourse in the 1970s, during which there was a strong government push for the prioritisation of locally derived conservation systems and practices.[31] These, however, were conceived as the responsibility of government agencies.

In particular, the ideas promoted by the UNESCO initiative were important for the conceptualisation of the museum development project (at least from the perspective of the writers), and as such the KHCMDP reflected an ideological position that asserted that heritage belongs to a community and therefore it follows that heritage values and expressions of cultural identity need to be prioritised by participants within the local community. In contemporary circumstances in Asia, the extent to which there can be an equitable and effective dispersal of responsibility for heritage conservation in diverse cultural, social and political circumstances across the region was, and remains, an important question. Even in Sarawak, where indigenous peoples form a majority of the population, the idea of local participation and agency (ownership, influence and/or control) in heritage-making and management raised a question about the degree to which it was achievable in a quite restrictive political and economic context. Nevertheless, the community museum development project provided an opportunity to follow the application of a people-centred approach to conservation that was conceived and pursued outside the official government museum network, with a particular aim to enhance agency and self-determination in the conservation and representation of Kelabit culture.

A recognition of the absolute importance of localised approaches to heritage conservation was essential to the project, but it was not intended that it be a statement concerning the superiority of local or international approaches to conservation. Local knowledge and circumstances may be essential to the sustainable conservation of cultural heritage, but due to the ways in which Kelabit culture has changed since WWII, this project was focused more upon the need for greater sensitivity to the hybrid experiences of indigenous cultures, and for the recognition of the influence this has in shaping contemporary heritage-making processes. Like other responses to the orthodoxies of international heritage practice in the region, this may also challenge the conventional concept of heritage 'authenticity'.[32] This is further challenged by the ingrained modernity of the community, and the desire to embrace contemporary forms of representation and communication. To an extent the community's approach to conservation and representation ought to be discussed as an expression of a form of cultural hybridity. This is a concept that Jan Nederveen Pieterse has argued 'foregrounds the openness and fluidity of identities', recognising 'the cut'n'mix zone of selves and others'.[33] In the project the RKS, while asserting its agency, has also sought the resources for heritage conservation from beyond the community, requiring the development of strategic partnerships both within and outside Sarawak. Internally too, the RKS has also walked a fine line in this organic and opportunistic process between the aspirations of an assertive outwardly looking leadership and the need for local community consultation. Pieterse sees hybridity as a matrix of power relations, and in this book, we echo this position and go some way towards explaining the context and the contributors that have a bearing on the project, to see the emergence of a hybrid concept of museology, design and representation.

It must be noted, however, the structure adopted in this chapter should not be read as a convenient binary split between a colonial and post-colonial thinking in Malaysia, because to an extent the case can be made that the origins of a more inclusive attitude towards the indigenous people of Sarawak and the emergence of participatory conservation processes lie in the post-WWII British colonial period. Furthermore, while the ideas and events that are discussed here may be reflected in the way in which the Kelabit community conceptualised their museum and cultural centre, it is also the case that the circumstances and processes through which the project occurred are highly significant.

Notes

1 Ivan Karp and Steven D. Lavine, *Exhibiting Cultures. The Poetics and Politics of Museum Display*, Smithsonian Institution Press, Washington and London, 1991.
2 Paul Walker, 'Institutional Audiences and Architectural Style, The Napier Museum', in Peter Scriver and Vikramaditya Prakash (eds), *Colonial Modernities, Building, Dwelling and Architecture in British India and Ceylon*, Routledge, London and New York, 2007, pp. 127–147.
3 Lucas Chin, Peter Kedit, Loh Chee Yin, Charles Leh, Ipoi Datan and Joseph Ingai, 'Development of the Sarawak Museum', *The Sarawak Museum Journal*, Vol.XXXII, No.53 (New Series), 1983, pp. 1–13, p. 5.
4 Iola Lenzi, *Museums of Southeast Asia*, Archipelago Press, Singapore, 2004, p. 104.
5 *The Directory of the Museums of ASEAN*, Singapore, 1988, p. 37.
6 Cherie McKeich, 'A "Barbaric Display of Oriental Magnificence": Indian Art at the Melbourne International Exhibition: 1880–1881', *Australian and New Zealand Journal of Art*, Vol.16, No.2, 2016, pp. 139–140.
7 Jonathan Sweet, *The Colonial Museum and UNESCO in the Asia Pacific Region*, PhD dissertation, Deakin University, 2010.

30 *Shaping Kelabit conservation processes*

8   John M. Mackenzie, *Museums and Empire: Natural History, Human Cultures and Colonial Identities*, Manchester University Press, Manchester, 2009.
9   Robert Reece, *The White Rajahs of Sarawak, a Borneo Dynasty*, Archipelago Press, Singapore, 2004, p. 53.
10 Gary Maitland, 'Sarawak Museum, the Museum of Borneo', *The Sarawak Museums Journal*, Vol.LIII, No.74, 1998, p. 96.
11 John M. Mackenzie, *Museums and Empire: Natural History, Human Cultures and Colonial Identities*, Manchester University Press, Manchester and New York, 2009, p. 113, p. 257.
12 For example, Robert Shelford, 'A Provisional Classification of the Swords of the Sarawak Tribes', *The Journal of the Anthropological Institute of Great Britain and Ireland*, Vol.31, January–June 1901, pp. 219–228.
13 See C.H. Read, 'Notes on a Collection of Gold Objects Found in Sarawak, in the Possession of His Highness the Rajah of Sarawak', *Man*, Vol.3, 1903, p. 6. And, The Pitt Rivers Museum, University of Oxford, which was one reference point for collection and display in the nineteenth century, currently exhibits human skulls and shrunken heads in a number of display cases. (Viewed and photographed, 11 January 2016.)
14 John M. Mackenzie, *Museums and Empire. Natural History, Human Cultures and Colonial Identities*, Manchester University Press, Manchester and New York, 2009, p. 257.
15 Judith M. Heimann, *The Most Offending Soul Alive: Tom Harrisson and His Remarkable Life*, University of Hawai'I Press, Honolulu, 1997.
16 T.H. Harrisson, 'The Oxford University Expedition to Sarawak, 1932', *The Geographical Journal*, Vol.82, No.5, 1933, pp. 385–406, p. 387.
17 Jonathan Sweet, Toyah Horman and Jennifer Rowe, 'The Community Museum and the Heritage of Conflict in the Kelabit Highlands, Sarawak, Malaysian Borneo', in Keir Reeves, Geffrey R. Bird, Laura James, Birger Stichelbaut and Jean Bourgeois (eds), *Battlefield Events: Landscape, Commemoration and Heritage*, Routledge, London and New York, pp. 189–199.
18 Barbara Harrisson, 'Tom Harrisson and the Uplands: A Summary of His Unpublished Ethnographic Papers', Reprinted from *Asian Perspectives*, Vol.XX, No.1, The University Press of Hawaii, 1979, pp. 1–7, p. 4.
19 Ibid, 1979, p. 4.
20 Carol Rubenstein, '"So Unable to Speak am I . . ." Sarawak Dayaks and Forms of Social Address in Song', *Asian Music: Journal of the Society for Asian Music*, Vol.21, No.2, 1990, pp. 1–37.
21 Carol Rubenstein, *Poems of Indigenous People of Sarawak: Some of the Songs and Chants, Parts I and II*, Sarawak Museums Journal, Special Monograph, Sarawak Museum, Kuching, 1973.
22 Judith M. Heimann, *The Most Offending Soul Alive: Tom Harrisson and His Remarkable Life*, University of Hawai'I Press, Honolulu, 1997, p. 271.
23 Lucy Bulan and David Labang, 'The Kelabit Harvest', *Sarawak Museums Journal*, Vol.XXVII, No.48, pp. 43–52.
24 B. Scanlon, *Sarawak in the Museum*, Borneo Literature Bureau, Revised Second Edition, 1968, p. iv. (First published 1961).
25 Begin with Lucas Chin, *Cultural Heritage of Sarawak*, Sarawak Museum, Kuching, 1980.
26 See, Heidi Tan (ed), *Museum-Community Partnerships: The Role of ASEAN Museums in the 21st Century*, National Heritage Board, Singapore, 2010.

27 United Nations, *Declaration on the Rights of Indigenous Peoples*, Resolution adopted by the General Assembly, 13 September 2007, p. 5, www.un.org/esa/socdev/unpfii/documents/DRIPS_en.pdf, accessed 13 December 2013. Malaysia voted in support of this Declaration.
28 United Nations, *Second International Decade of the World's Indigenous People*, Resolution adopted by the General Assembly, 22 December 2004. http://undesadspd.org/IndigenousPeoples/SecondDecade.aspx, accessed 13 December 2013.
29 UNESCO, *Indigenous Peoples*, www.unesco.org/new/en/indigenous-peoples/sustainable-development-and-environmental-change/, accessed 13 December 2013.
30 R.A. Engelhardt and P. Rumball Rogers (2003), *Hoi An Protocols for Best Conservation Practice in Asia. [Electronic Resource]: Professional Guidelines for Assuring and Preserving the Authenticity of Heritage Sites in the Context of the Cultures of Asia*, UNESCO, Asia and Pacific Regional Bureau for Education, Bangkok, 2009.
31 A.R. bin M. Ibrahim, 'Conservation in Malaysia', *Proceedings of the ASPAC Experts Meeting on Preservation of Cultural Heritage, May 31 – June 4, 1971*, Cultural and Social Centre for the Asian and Pacific Region, Seoul, 1972, p. 78.
32 See, Gamini Wijesuriya and Jonathan Sweet (eds), *Revisiting Authenticity in the Asian Context*, ICCROM, Rome, Forthcoming.
33 Jan Nederveen Pieterse, 'Multiculturalism and Museums: Discourse about Others in the Age of Globalization', in Gerard Corsane (ed), *Heritage, Museum and Galleries, an Introductory Reader*, Routledge, London, 1997, pp. 163–183, p. 173.

3 History, knowledge and the representation of identity

Introduction

Creating a clear conception of heritage and identity requires looking to the past to help define and prioritise the values that the community may want to conserve in the future. For the members of the RKS this process began very personally in the 1960s and 1970s when as young educated professionals they began to ask questions about their indigenous culture and wrestle with their increasing hybridity. For this generation in particular, the experience of belonging to a non-Malay indigenous community and additionally of being committed Christians in the new nation state of Malaysia was a profound change to that of their grandparents who lived in entirely different circumstances and according to different values before and during WWII. The dramatic changes in the post-war years raised interest in the question of identity, which led to a gradual process of research and community action over a number of decades and subsequently to the creation of the RKS and the Kelabit Highlands Community Museum Development Project.

During these decades, some young members of the community encountered western epistemology at school and at university, and they began to adopt the methodologies of historical, archaeological and anthropological research. They started to identify and prioritise clues in their society to assist with piecing together an understanding of cultural, economic or spiritual practices of the past. There were few written records from the colonial period, and more importantly there were no written chronicles generated by the community. This raised the question of the extent to which the Kelabit youth were able to draw upon authenticated historical sources of information, upon which to base their conclusions about the history and values of Kelabit culture.

In the nineteenth and twentieth centuries, the absence of written records meant that the collecting and research of material culture was the dominant scientific framework for researching the indigenous peoples of Sarawak.

This is clearly represented by the collecting activity supported by personnel based at the Sarawak Museum. However, in the 1970s the collections at the museum were patchy and items often lacked enough information to enrich an understanding of the associated values, leaving many unanswered questions. Historians and anthropologists (including Kelabit researchers) after WWII looked to the local knowledge that was being disseminated through oral traditions (storytelling) and performance, and documented these activities in English and local languages. In 1979, recent university graduates Robert Lian and Robert Saging contributed an article to the *Borneo Research Bulletin* that was titled, 'An ethno-history of the Kelabit tribe of Sarawak: a brief look at the Kelabit tribe before World War II and after'.[1] This was amongst the first cluster of published historical accounts emanating from within the Kelabit community, along with David Labang and Lucy Bulan's article on the Kelabit rice harvest. The group of young Kelabit scholars used a range of methodologies to begin to establish an authoritative account of the pre-contact history and continuities in their culture.

The relative paucity of records and the lack of a public collection in the Kelabit Highlands, including historical material in particular, was therefore an important aspect of investigation in the first phase of this project. Fieldwork conducted in Bario confirmed that despite the extensive loss of pre-WWII material culture (largely as a consequence of Christianity and the vanquishing of evil spirits), most Kelabit longhouses contained many interesting historical items. These ranged from bronze gongs, which were used ceremonially and for communication, varieties of handheld agricultural tools and hunting weapons, as well as other personal keepsakes. The inventory of these keepsakes included items of Chinese ceramics, and photographs and memorabilia that have been handed down through families. Researchers in the KHCMDP encouraged the participation of the community in the investigation of the history and values of these things, and many owners and family members discussed the meanings of their possessions openly. In some cases, the respondents were able to share very personal stories about the history and associated values of their items. Nevertheless, the breadth of their responses was often quite narrow. While a professional heritage consultant undertaking a material culture analysis may have more confidently articulated the aesthetic, historic, social or spiritual significance of these items, in general the explanations provided by the owners provided little contextual information and revealed a fairly limited account of history. This raised an important question about the prism or framework through which the community will engage with the stories and meanings associated with their treasured items. In addition, it raised a question as to the basis and means through which decisions about the relative significance of material that might be incorporated into the official representation of Kelabit identity would be made. To contextualise these issues, this chapter reviews some examples of the past research into Kelabit culture and discusses issues concerning the use of historical sources.

Geographical and social parameters

For most of their history, the mobility of the Kelabit was largely restricted to the Highlands because the route to the coast of northeast Borneo was obstructed by the lack of navigable waterways – meaning that it took a month to walk to the sea. This meant that the Kelabit people were amongst the last of the indigenous people of Borneo to have contact with Europeans, and therefore there are very few references to their society in the nineteenth century and during the government of the Brookes Dynasty (the so-called 'White Rajas' of Sarawak) who governed between 1841 and 1941. Robert Pringle undertook research into the status of indigenous people during this period and found that while members of the Iban tribes were actively involved in the Brookes administration, the Kelabit 'remained beyond effective contact'.[2] With little external intervention, the community conserved its own culture; knowledge was transmitted orally and through a combination of longstanding conventions that included art, craft and design, spiritual, agricultural and hunting practices and music and dance. In the years immediately before WWII, access to the Kelabit Highlands remained problematic, as Werner F. Schneeberger, a consultant geologist for the Batavian Oil Company, discovered in 1939. He reported that a round trip to the 'Kerayan-Kalabit highland' (sic) would take at least six weeks to two months, and that rather than visit his report had therefore relied on information and maps provided by the Netherlands Indies Forest Department and Sarawak Oilfields Limited. The American Geographical Society published his report on the geography of the region in 1945 (even though he had not actually reached the Highlands) in the expectation that it was of 'potential interest'.[3] This enterprise, however was premature because at that time Sarawak was occupied by the Japanese army, and British and Australian servicemen were engaged with the Kelabit in fighting them in north Borneo. In 1949, Tom Harrisson, who was based in the Kelabit Highlands in 1944 and 1945, underscored the remote locations of the Kelabit longhouses which he said were located 'in the least accessible area at the headwaters of the Baram River'.[4]

Due to his personal operational experience in the Highlands, Harrisson was an expert on the ways in which the Kelabit navigated the geography of the region, and his writings about geography, life and society in the Highlands provide a very important source for understanding Kelabit culture in the mid-twentieth century. In addition to the difficult terrain, he reported in

1949 that they were constrained in their movements by 'the intricate pattern of head-hunting', which also contributed to their isolation.[5] The complex interactions the Kelabit had with other tribes, which included trade but also warfare, had implications for this museum development project. In particular, in considering the scope of heritage interpretation it suggested that there was a need to discuss inter-tribal relationships with a view to articulating what was distinctive about Kelabit identity. Nowadays headhunting has been erased from the memory of the Kelabit people and there may be good reasons for down-playing its cultural significance. But as Harrisson realised, to a degree the historical and cultural values associated with headhunting, which was widespread amongst the Borneo tribes, offered a way of foregrounding Kelabit distinctiveness. Harrisson theorised that the difficult geography of the interior limited the possibilities for the Kelabit to engage in headhunting, and as a consequence it was less practiced,[6] although it was evident during WWII, when the heads of Japanese soldiers were displayed in the village. Peter Metcaff has researched headhunting practices more recently and has suggested that it had a far greater prevalence in the lowlands.[7] Thus, while it is well documented that trophy heads were displayed in Kelabit longhouses and invested with sacred meaning, the community today may feel that their engagement with headhunting was not as important to their culture as it was to some more active tribes. In terms of material evidence there may have been substantially fewer of these trophies in existence in the Bario longhouse in the 1950s and 1960s than there were in other longhouses, and this (along with their fragility and association with pagan practices) in turn may explain why the authors saw no surviving examples in Bario. Nevertheless, this underscores a question about the weight of significance given to past pagan social and spiritual practices in the museum's heritage interpretation.

The isolation of the Kelabit longhouses also contributed to the complex relationship they had with their more immediate neighbours, particularly the Penan. These people were nomadic forest dwellers and predominately hunters, in contrast to the Kelabit who maintained some agricultural practices. In recent years, the Penan have been forced out of forest areas in the region due to logging and have been resettled in close proximity to Bario.[8] They produce highly attractive woven handicrafts that are sold in the market. During this project the history and current circumstances of the Penan also raised a challenging question about their inclusion or exclusion in the museum's heritage interpretation. The issue is centred on the extent to which the Kelabit are willing to engage in a discussion about how their identity has been shaped through their longstanding and complex historical relationships (including headhunting) with their indigenous neighbours.

Material culture and intangible heritage in the Highlands

To begin to understand the relationships between the interpretation of Kelabit culture and the historical record, we need to appreciate the influence of Tom Harrisson during the immediate post-war years. The Kelabit were amongst the last of the indigenous tribes of North Borneo to come into contact with the colonial government. With very few exceptions during the 1930s, external contact was limited and much of the documentation about Kelabit history and traditional practices begins from the middle of the twentieth century with WWII. British Commander Colonel John Chapman-Walker commented in 1949 that Harrisson established 'a greater degree of control and administration of the natives than had ever been established in the interior of Borneo before the war, or was ever likely to be established for many years to come'.[9] This had important ramifications for heritage conservation after WWII, when Sarawak was an official British Colony (1946–1962). It was during this period that Harrisson wrote extensively about his personal engagement with Kelabit culture in his important memoir, *World Within. A Borneo Story*, which provides an absorbing account of the wartime operations and describes life inside Bario Asal (the longhouse) in detail.[10] As a consequence of his personal experience and professional expertise, Harrisson became an important advocate for the conservation of indigenous tangible and intangible cultural heritage in Borneo, and an important agent in promoting the role of museums for cultural development in Southeast Asia.[11]

The opportunity for Harrisson to maintain his personal friendships with Kelabit leaders and further his research interests in the Kelabit Highlands came when he was appointed to the position of Government Ethnologist and Museum Curator at the Sarawak Museum in Kuching. During his tenure, he brought a dynamic approach to the curatorship of the museum and began to rebuild the reputation of the organisation, fractured and weakened during WWII. At the start of his tenure the range of artefacts of Kelabit origin was piecemeal and unrepresentative, because for the most part these were fortuitous acquisitions rather than the result of systematic collecting. The scope of material was very underdeveloped, and this reflected the isolation and inaccessibility of the tribe. Nevertheless, an opportunistic acquisition was reported in 1933 in *MAN*, the journal of the Royal Anthropological Institute of Great Britain and Ireland, as a member of the Sarawak Civil Service had somehow obtained two Kelabit baskets in the Baram River region.[12]

Nowadays the residents of Bario maintain long held attachments to many kinds of objects, and in part this may be a legacy of the attention Harrisson and others paid to documenting the material culture of the region. These items include ancestral heirlooms of historical significance, some of which may be very old indeed. These came into longhouses through established trade routes through Brunei and Sabah that were active to the coast. This is supported by historical evidence concerning the transaction of cultural material that confirms that locally obtained and imported objects were highly valued possessions. For example, the anthropologist and collector A.C. Haddon reported in 1900 that the local people had vested spiritual significance in stone implements for which they had a 'high regard' and with which they were reluctant to part.[13] Similarly, Harrisson reported in 1968 that 'it was a big thing' for him to receive a rare Chinese ceramic vessel (c. fifteenth century) from the Kelabit Headman, T.K. Anvi, of the longhouse Pa Bengar, which was used in the ritual drinking of rice-wine.[14]

The significance of material culture was reconfirmed during the KHC-MDP in a community consultation meeting held in Pa Lungun, which is a four-hour walk from Bario. The discussion explored the idea that the community would be involved in the interpretation process at the museum through providing items for short-term loan around which they could contribute their own stories. In part this approach was canvassed because it was seen to enhance community involvement but also because it was not feasible for the museum to create its own collection (in the short-term), and there were also obvious issues with transporting exhibition or loan material from outside the Highlands to the site. At the meeting the strategy was misunderstood and it was assumed that the project team was treasure hunting. In response, the importance of heirlooms to the Pa Lungun families was asserted by a village spokesman, who reiterated that this material was of high personal significance. As he said,

> the question of whether it will be on loan or whether it would be donated, for example. Like us, this is our heirloom, they are brought down from our grandparents, so for us to part with, I think it's a great loss to us as well, because we also are talking about *our* Kelabit history, *our* Kelabit culture, based on all these artefacts.[15]

Although there was some local misunderstanding, the heartfelt reconfirmation that these artefacts were symbolically associated with their ancestors more broadly reflected the role of material culture to contemporary culture.

Some of these items, in particular ceramics and ornamental beads (that were most commonly made in Southern India and China) were commodities that gained high social significance in Kelabit culture prior to colonial contact and still embody tangible and intangible heritage values for longhouse communities. The significance of these artefacts can be viewed in a number of ways; the first is illustrated by the use of beads to make apparel and jewellery. This is the result of the continuity of craft traditions that have contributed to the preservation of traditional knowledge through formalised processes of social interaction. In the history of museums, the recognition and discussion of the relationships between materials, processes and designs – at the core of which is knowledge and intangible cultural heritage – is integral to contextualising and interpreting objects within an exhibition space. The potential use of this material in the museum was particularly appealing to the Kelabit during the project, and reflects a more widespread curatorial appreciation of the connections between tangible and intangible heritage. For example, Marilena Alivizatou has argued that through engaging with traditional knowledge and processes (intangible cultural heritage), curators are able to facilitate a wider and deeper interpretation of the artefacts on display.[16] A current revival in beading and the safeguarding of traditional knowledge, designs and skilled practices has been supported by past research and in more recent years by the direct actions of the community. In the Kelabit Highlands women make items of jewellery and costume for sale to tourists, but they also make the distinctive skullcaps, which they wear. This contemporary work draws upon a distinct range of patterns, some of which are known from older examples and documented records.[17] In 1951, Harrisson described how he obtained an insight into how traditional knowledge was transmitted between generations, and thus supported the continuity of craft practices:

> I have spent the last five years sitting among the people carving wood, working patterns in iron, making fascinating hats or necklaces of beads. I sat in their houses, and they in mine. Once having acquired a common language, I was able to listen to the most extensive explanations of what they were doing and why.[18]

Harrisson was engaged in a western-led anthropological activity which afforded the outside world with his interpretation of Kelabit culture, but his work also provided the Kelabit with a direct experience of heritage-making processes, and as Sarawak became more accessible to international visitors, the possibilities of cultural development through tourism driven artistic production. This raised the question of the extent to which the meaning invested in these items was diluted by their value as commodities.

In the late 1920s, Bronislaw Malinowski argued that anthropology was intended to assist colonial governments to make more humane decisions concerning the native peoples they administered.[19] In this colonial context, Harrisson's concern for indigenous art and craft practice may be seen as an example of this kind of 'practical anthropology'. It is clear that he claimed a certain legitimacy to interpret these practices, and that his access to knowledge was in a great part derived from his colonial authority. He was, however, equally aware that Christianity and westernisation posed a direct threat to the continuity of intangible heritage in Sarawak, rupturing the processes through which traditional knowledge had been passed from one generation to the next, and also through undermining the value of spiritual beliefs or meanings embodied in the practices and in the objects created.

This posed a challenge for Harrisson because despite his position within the British colonial administration, he was concerned to prosecute his high regard for the indigenous people of Sarawak. He therefore tried to find a way to align his work in Borneo with that of the new international agency UNESCO and a broader emerging ethos, which was to promote the nexus between education, culture and development. In 1949 he wrote to John Bowers, Head of the Department of Fundamental Education, UNESCO, Paris,

> Julian Huxley [the first Director General of UNESCO 1946–1948] gave me your name as someone interested in the preservation, and exhibition of native crafts, a subject with which I am much concerned as Government Ethnologist and Curator of the Sarawak Museum in Borneo. I hope to be over in Paris in June, and was wondering if you would be available then for a talk.[20]

At this time, the idea of creating a UNESCO Indigenous Arts Program was being discussed, and it is clear that Harrisson had become aware of this through his contact with Julian Huxley. At a meeting held in 1949 the delegates posited the view (that also echoed the work of Malinowski) that the preservation of traditional arts and crafts for its own sake was not an ambitious enough aim in itself for such a program. Specifically, the program should also be focused on the preservation and encouragement of indigenous arts and crafts activity which might also have a role in poverty alleviation in developing countries.[21]

It was an ambitious idea in 1949 but clearly there was a trade in hand crafted indigenous items in Sarawak in the 1950s. After Malaysian independence, the business of indigenous arts and crafts was actively supported and promoted by the Sarawak Government. The State Economic Development Corporation established the organisation *Sarakraf*, which a tourist guide to Kuching reported in 2003 aimed 'to help develop Sarawak's handicrafts industry and at the same time improve the economic situation of rural craftspeople'. *The Official Guide to Kuching* also assured visitors that 'Most of their products are guaranteed, "made in Sarawak", and you can be sure the producers have been fairly rewarded for their creative efforts'.[22] This kind of government support and commercial promotion are now part of an expansive tourism system in Sarawak and may have delivered some benefits to rural people. Nevertheless, the commodification of indigenous art and craft had also raised questions about the agency and representation of indigenous people in the process. For example, the academic Dave Cooper described a postcard from Sarawak that depicted 'a Kelabit warrior', writing that 'His tabard and headdress are so pristine, and obviously of some value due to the intricacy of the work, that we suspect that they were donned particularly for the portrait'.[23] Thus, he argued this presented an illusion of the 'authentic primitive' (which he recognised was increasingly widespread in tourism commodities). This type of product certainly contributed to the continuity of craft practices, but the traditional style headdress and jewellery were used to construct an image of a Kelabit warrior and offered a somewhat distorted view of Kelabit life in the late twentieth century.[24]

Such representation needs to be distinguished from the cultural practices that Harrisson witnessed and documented before the age of mass tourism. The process of creating headdresses and other items of jewellery made from beads and bone and feathers was of social and spiritual significance, highly ritualised. To a certain extent this is now reflected in the safeguarding of these well provenanced items as family heirlooms. The Sarawak Museum curator Lucas Chin reported in 1980, for example, that 'the Kelabit seldom part with their beads except in times of starvation or to settle an inheritance dispute'.[25] It may also be distinguished from community efforts to promote the tradition of beading that is represented by events such as the *Borneo International Beads Conference*, which was held in Kuching in 2013. This included a program of academic papers discussing the traditions of beading and a presentation by an RKS committee member, Dr Poline Bala, Head of the Department of Anthropology and Sociology, University of Malaysia (Sarawak), on 'Kelabit Bead Values in a Changing World'.[26]

Another kind of significance may be accorded to those objects that are historically and culturally linked to previous generations. Old Chinese ceramic jars illustrate this kind of value very well, as they are still proudly conserved by a number of Kelabit families. In the nineteenth and twentieth centuries, colonial anthropologists and administrators observed that for a range of reasons these vessels were sought after across Borneo by many indigenous tribes. Charles Hose, a Brookes era District Officer who was working as a trouble shooter in northwest Sarawak, noted that the Iban 'have a habit of *collecting* large vases of china-ware, which they prize highly'.[27] But, despite the rarity of these jars, Hose was apparently able to secure a jar from a Kelabit longhouse that was presented to the Sarawak Museum in 1892, the earliest recorded object of Kelabit origin in the collection (accession number 792).[28] District Officers also provided interesting information about how these jars were used: In 1913 Owen Rutter, who was based in

North Borneo (now Sabah), observed that for certain festivals the coastal Dusuns invested their jars with spiritual significance and arranged them in 'the house, surrounded by smaller jars, and wrapped in cloths of gold and hung with old bead necklaces'.[29] This may have been a very longstanding practice, however by the 1920s it was observed that these jars were disappearing from these communities, having been either sold or destroyed under the influence of the Roman Catholic Mission.[30]

In the isolated Kelabit Highlands, the jars were still visible and valued after WWII: Harrisson writing in 1959 that these 'dragon jars' (so-called because of the stylised dragons with which they are decorated) he saw were traditionally of substantial trade value, and were worth a human slave or a buffalo and were sometimes the focus of disputes between family members.[31] They were also being used in various communal longhouse ceremonies as vessels for brewing beer and wine. This enabled Harrison to theorise about the external origins of some Kelabit cultural practices, writing that 'the massive alcoholic feasts which play such a big part in Kelabit life today probably date from the arrival of the Chinese jars . . . as the techniques for distilling spirit (arrack) and rice beer (borak) had been quite recently learned from the Chinese on visits to the coast'.[32] These feasts were perhaps also a legacy of other traditional ceremonies that used Chinese-origin ceramic vessels. As Lucas Chin explained, during the 'Kelabit head-rite' painted cups in the form of a duck, crayfish or crane were 'used in making libations to the enemies' heads and then in passing rice-wine (borak) round amongst aristocrats'.[33] Another group of ceramic pots were also used in association with these head-rites; and these 'were hung up with the enemies' heads [from the rafters of the longhouse] so as to obtain some of the powerful qualities of the heads', then sealed with wooden or antler stoppers to preserve 'their spirits'.[34]

By the early 1950s, however, traditional spiritual activities were declining as Christianity and western education became more influential in the region. It is likely that the documentary photographs made by Hedda Morrison during one of her visits to Bario Asal in the mid-1950s included a photograph which captured one of the last authentic feasts showing the use of the 'dragon jars', although it is also possible that the scene was especially staged for the camera.[35] It is clear, however, that due to the change in Kelabit circumstances in the decades after WWII, the values and meanings accorded to the 'dragon jars' and other Chinese-origin ceramic vessels through their association with ceremonial activities and specific family histories had changed. The details about the use and provenance of the jars currently held in the longhouses of Bario are often less than clear, although at least four of these jars are clearly visible in another of Morrison's photographs of the interior of Bario Asal from 1957.[36] In most cases these jars have been carefully preserved and are still displayed as proud symbols of past authority and wealth of high status Kelabit families. Sometimes these jars are arranged in ways that seem to echo the Dusun display of jars described by Rutter, and although this may be unintentional, their preciousness accords them a high degree of heritage significance.

Jars are also on occasion to be found housed in less conspicuous circumstances such as the storage shed cared for by Walter Paran. Paran told the journalist Karen Coates that his jar was used for the storage of rice; but Paran said that he really knew very little about its history and significance, and had no stories from his parents to share: He lamented that 'we forgot to ask ... that's a big mistake for us. That is why we are losing our history ... and that's why our children, they don't know'.[37] The evident changes in the heritage values accorded to these items over a few generations from economic, social and spiritual functions, to a greater emphasis on aesthetic or simply commercial value, raises a number of questions for the process of heritage interpretation that are still unresolved. This includes the extent to which the scope of the available knowledge is sufficient to engage with the layers of meaning embodied in the history of these artefacts. Furthermore, the research into the material culture evident in Bario undertaken for the Kelabit museum project revealed a question around the extent to which highly aesthetic objects will eclipse the consideration of utilitarian objects, and the less glorious stories associated with them. These are items related to agricultural practices or to the experiences of the non-elite families (including slaves and recent itinerant workers) that have figured in shaping Kelabit history.

Notes

1 Robert Lian and Robert Saging, 'An Ethno-History of the Kelabit Tribe of Sarawak: A Brief Look at the Kelabit Tribe Before World War II and After', *Borneo Research Bulletin*, Vol.11, No.1, 1979, pp. 14–19.
2 Robert Pringle, *Rajahs and Rebels: The Ibans of Sarawak Under the Brooke Rule, 1841–1941*, Cornell University Press, New York, 1970, p. 320.
3 Werner F. Schneeberger, 'The Kerayan–Kalabit Highland of Central Northest Borneo', *Geographical Review*, Vol.35, No.4, October 1945, pp. 544–562, pp. 545–546.
4 Tom Harrisson, 'Outside Influences on the Culture of the Kelabits of North Central Borneo', *Journal of the Polynesian Society*, Vol.58, No.3, 1949, p. 91.
5 Ibid, 1949, pp. 91–111, p. 91.
6 Tom Harrisson, *World Within: A Borneo Story*, The Cresset Press, London, 1959, p. 92.
7 Peter Metcalf, 'Images of Headhunting', in Janet Hoskins (ed), *Headhunting and the Social Imagination in Southeast Asia*, Stanford University Press, Stanford, 1996, pp. 248–290. p. 265.

8 Evelyne Hong, *Natives of Sarawak, Survival in Borneo's Vanishing Forests*, Institut Masyarakat, Malaysia, 1987, pp. 89–90.
9 Lord Rennel of Rodd, John Chapman-Walker, Woodrow Wyatt and E.A. Shackleton, 'Explorations in Central Borneo: Discussion', *The Geographical Journal*, Vol.114, No.4/6, 1949, p. 150.
10 Tom Harrisson, *World Within: A Borneo Story*, The Cresset Press, London, 1959.
11 Jonathan Sweet, *The Colonial Museum and UNESCO in the Asia Pacific Region*, PhD Dissertation, Deakin University, 2010.
12 J.C. Swayne, 'Borneo: Technology. A Kelabit Basket', *MAN*, No.4/5, January 1933, pp. 10–11, p. 10.
13 A.C. Haddon, 'Relics of the Stone Age of Borneo', *The Journal of the Anthropological Institute of Great Britain and Ireland*, Vol.30, 1900, pp. 71–72.
14 Tom Harrisson, 'The Kelabit "Duck Ewer" in the Sarawak Museum', *Sarawak Museum Journal*, Vol.XVI, 1968.
15 Simon Wilmot, World Within No More, VEA Australia, New Zealand, Bendigo, Victoria, 2013.
16 Marilena Alivizatou, *Intangible Heritage and the Museum: New Perspectives on Cultural Preservation*, Left Coast Press, Walnut Creek, CA., 2012.
17 See, Charles Hose, *Natural Man, a Record from Borneo*, Oxford University Press, Singapore 1988, pp. 168–175. (First published 1926).
18 Tom Harrisson, 'Art for One's Own Sake', *MAN*, No.244–246, October 1951, pp. 146–147, p. 146.
19 Erve Chamber, 'Applied Ethnography', in Norman K. Denzin and Yvonna S. Lincoln (eds), *Handbook of Qualitative Research*, Second Edition, Sage Publications, Thousand Oaks, CA, 2000, pp. 851–869, p. 853.
20 Tom Harrisson, *Letter to J. Bowers UNESCO Concerning Native Crafts*, UNESCO Archive, Paris, May 9, 1949.
21 *Documents Related to UNESCO's Indigenous Arts Program*, UNESCO, Paris, 1949.
22 *The Official Kuching Guide 2003*, Travelcom Asia, Eighth Edition, 2002, p. 62.
23 Dave Cooper, 'Portraits of Paradise: Themes and Images for the Tourist Industry', *Southeast Asian Journal of Social Science*, Vol.22, Cultural Studies in the Asia Pacific, 1994, pp. 144–160, p. 156.
24 Ibid, 1994, p. 156.
25 Lucas Chin, *Cultural Heritage of Sarawak*, Sarawak Museum, Kuching, 1980, p. 50.
26 Borneo International Beads Conference 2013, http://crafthub.com.my/?page_id=36, accessed 11 October 2017.
27 Charles Hose, *Natural Man: A Record from Borneo*, Oxford University Press, Singapore, 1988. (First published 1926), p. 89.
28 Cited in Ian J. Ewart, *The Documented History of the Kelabits of Northern Sarawak*, unpublished, unpaginated, www.arch.cam.ac.uk/research/projects/cultured-rainforest/crp-files/2009-ewart-the-documented-history-of-the-kelabits.pdf, accessed 3 November 2107.
29 Owen Rutter, *The Pagans of North Borneo*, Oxford University Press, Singapore, 1985. (First published 1929), p. 242.
30 Ibid, 1985, p. 241.
31 Tom Harrisson, *World Within: A Borneo Story*, The Cresset Press, London, 1959, p. 107.

32 Tom Harrisson, 'Outside Influences on the Culture of the Kelabits of North Central Borneo', *The Journal of the Polynesian Society*, Vol.59, No.3, September 1949, pp. 91–111. p. 97.
33 Lucas Chin, *Cultural Heritage of Sarawak*, Sarawak Museum, Kuching, 1980, p. 30.
34 Ibid, 1980, p. 30.
35 Hedda Morrison, *Sarawak*, MacGibbon & Kee, London, 1957, p. 278.
36 Ibid, 1957, p. 275.
37 Quoted in Karen Coates, 'The Landscape of Memory', *Archaeology*, Vol.67, No.2, March/April 2014, pp. 55–59, 61, p. 59.

4 Museum development and tourism
Identifying authenticity and representation

Introduction

Since Malaysian independence, government museums have maintained dominance over the representation of indigenous people. In 1964, the Department of Aboriginal Affairs established the Orang Asli Museum in Kuala Lumpur, which opened to the public on September 29, 1987.[1] In 2000, it was upgraded in a new building that Iola Lenzi believes 'provides [visitors with] an insight into the history, traditions and material culture of the indigenous tribal population of Malaysia'.[2] Nevertheless, we argue that the administrative link between the government department and the representation of indigenous peoples produces a reductive representation of a diverse range of indigenous peoples, and that the museum may implicitly act to emphasise the separation of indigenous peoples from the Malay Muslim majority. Indigenous people have little agency in museum representation and very little influence on how their culture or values are represented. In contrast, through KHCMDP the Kelabit community pursued a process of self-reflection that was focused on the articulation of its own values and identity.

Thus the RKS pursued an interest in reflective museology, and the project necessitated the discussion of some aligned critical questions. These centred on the relationship between the role of museums in cultural and economic development and the issue of creating and maintaining 'authenticity' in the representation of values and identity. This chapter contextualises the discussion within a broader reflection upon the relationships between these factors in Sarawak, where the representation of non-Malay indigenous people has largely been undertaken by government organisations focused on tourism services. The synergy between cultural representation and the tourism system (often masquerading as 'cultural tourism') has raised concerns within indigenous communities because of the inevitable undermining of authenticity. To provide an example we look at the Sarawak Cultural

Village, which is a strong reference point for the Kelabit. We then discuss the complexity of indigenous agency, authenticity and tourism with an aim to understanding how it may be possible for the Kelabit people to achieve more than a narrow commodification of their culture.

The problem of indigenous agency: museums, identity representation and the tourism system

Evident in tightly regulated government museum programs are systemic political and religious biases that mitigate against the promotion of indigenous values that retard the respectful integration of non-Malay values. Jinn Winn Chong has argued that the Malaysian government's approach to ethnic diversity and national cohesion has more often favoured 'the accommodation and reorientation of non-Malays', such as non-Malay indigenous people, over concepts and strategies of 'integration and assimilation'. This has diluted the government's ability to achieve 'the construction of a substantive unified national culture within the state'.[3] Chong has observed that in practice this has also led to a very pragmatic and superficial interpretation of what constitutes or is defined as 'cultural heritage', which is reduced to those values which are associated with a constructed notion of Malaysian identity. He has argued that in circumstances where tangible things and intangible practices cannot be seen to embody Malay Muslim values, these are largely reconstituted as 'economic interests, entertainment, and community activity'; and thus, the concept of cultural heritage is 'rarely held out as a core and immutable essence of a people's identity'.[4] This has had the effect of disrupting any deep-seated commitment to indigenous values in non-Malay indigenous people, perhaps most evident in the ways in which government owned or sponsored cultural tourism products often claim to be authentic expressions of the culture of non-Malay indigenous peoples when authenticity cannot be guaranteed.

This dislocation raises questions about where authentic values may be located or expressed in a hybrid and changing Kelabit society. In the first place this can be illustrated in the growth of the village of Bario since 1945. Despite its relative isolation in the Kelabit Highlands of northeast Borneo (East Malaysia), where the town is located 1000 metres above sea level and close to the border of Indonesia, there has been a steady change in the townscape that reflects the social change that has occurred. In the 1940s, the isolated and sprawling Bario Asal was nestled in the foothills of the Tamabo Mountains, surrounded by bands of scrub and grassland and virgin jungle. While the longhouse had been reconstructed many times, it had featured in the landscape for centuries. The present building that was built in the 1970s continues to evolve and has a much different relationship to the surrounding landscape. The physical structure also reflects the changing expectations of the inhabitants, with one family recently adding a private modern bathroom to their quarters. In 2012, architect Ian Ewart observed that the valley in which it is situated now includes 'fifteen or twenty other buildings, including a large school and Christian church' which are 'all centred around a football pitch instead of the main longhouse'.[5] Other modern buildings may now be added to the list, including a base hospital and even more recently the completed Kelabit Highlands Community Museum. In other words, over the last two or three generations, as Bario has developed as the principle market town of the Kelabit Highlands, there has been a substantial shift in the prominence and authority of the Bario Asal as the sole cultural and administrative centre of the community. Thus, the association of the longhouse with the custodianship of traditional values and practices has been challenged by the development of the town more broadly and the interests of other members of the community.

The evolution of the built environment in the Kelabit Highlands reflects many other shifts that have also occurred in contemporary Kelabit culture. Very significant, for example, is the change in the way people have chosen to live, moving from living in communal longhouses to private houses and embracing new materials in the design of buildings as they have become more readily available. According to Ewart, these changes reflect the Kelabit people's involvement in a 'continual process of exploration, engagement and mutual creation'.[6]

In addition, the substitution of traditional agricultural practices in the town in favour of mechanised rice farming has had an aesthetic impact on the environment and social consequences for the local people. The rationalisation of this shift illustrates the fine line between conservation and development that has unnerved some community members. It has been claimed for example that mechanised rice farming has both heritage conservation and economic benefits as the introduction of 'mechanised rice farming has made tremendous inroads into re-igniting the ancient art of producing the famed Bario Rice' and 'has restored abandoned rice farms and helped farmers increase their yield'.[7] Currently, mechanised farming is championed with aerial views of the rice fields on the website of the project's backers, the Ceria Group (Bario Ceria), along with the types of machines that are used.[8] These changes in agricultural practices (that commenced during the KHCMDP) underscored the need to address the significance of the interdependence between nature and culture in the Kelabit Highlands and the implications this might have for the representation of Kelabit identity, before the intangible links to the past are all but erased.

In recent years some members of the Kelabit community have adopted contemporary modes of living that reflect their individual wealth, but these same people have also feared the erosion of social cohesion and the accompanying loss of the ways and means of sharing traditional knowledge. They have openly expressed the need to address these threats while also respecting the need for economic and social development in the town; and they have acted by seeking to define and anchor a notion of Kelabit identity in the conceptualisation of a community museum. In this book, we situate the creation of the KHCMDP in a deep-seated anxiety steaming from the ways modernity has threatened to erode the memory of the past and to fragment the Kelabit community. As is widely accepted by social scientists, 'a full sense of community is fictional and fragile' and 'ever vulnerable to external threats and internal fissures'.[9] So, in part, the Kelabit people have been proactive in seeking redress through a range of initiatives. These have included the annual *Presta Nukenen* (Food Festival) that started in 2005, and which the writer and photographer Nikki Lugun has stated aims 'to recover and preserve traditional methods of indigenous edible plants and safeguard local plants and animal species', and which additionally 'serves to draw the close-knit community even closer together'.[10] In effect initiatives such as the museum have been part of a 'bottom-up' approach to conservation and social and economic development orchestrated by the RKS.

Tourism has become integral to many heritage sites and museums around the globe, but in this small community, at least hypothetically, it may have a disproportionate influence on the design and management of cultural events. The KHCMDP provided a framework for the self-reflective articulation of Kelabit identity, but the RKS also saw the project as a development opportunity. The museum was envisioned as a gateway to the Kelabit Highlands, and it is hoped that it will enhance the existing civic complex in Bario, which is used for congregation and recreation, and that social and economic capital will be generated from the synergies between cultural tourism and heritage conservation (in unison with the Food Festival). In part this aim extended the argument for tourism initiatives that were promoted by consultant Roger W. Harris, which included cultural programs and performances as part of an evolving strategy of integrated community development.[11] This strategy also reflected the success that other indigenous communities have attained in countries such as Canada through enacting programs that have utilised their living heritage in an effort to assist with the reconnection of locals to their own sense of belonging and invigorate a pride of place. Such programs have provided ways of fostering sustainable forms of cultural, social and economic development, through engagement with business and tourism.[12] A challenge for the RKS, however, was and remains the extent to which the museum or cultural centre might provide more than a narrow commodification of Kelabit culture, or be swallowed up by a powerful national tourism system.

The Sarawak Cultural Village

To understand the risks posed to the RKS initiative, it is necessary to see the museum project from another perspective and to discuss the operations of the Sarawak Cultural Village (SCV), which is a model of a type of indigenous representation that has influenced the vision of the RKS. The SCV was established in 1990 and is owned by the Sarawak Economic Development Corporation (SEDC). This is a statutory body established under the laws of the State of Sarawak, but the operations of the SCV also come under the purview of the Federal Government of Malaysia through the Federal Ministry of Finance. It is an example of a type of cultural representation, in which natives are seen by visitors to be engaged in traditional activities in a traditional setting. This form has evolved from western exhibition practices of the nineteenth century and been taken up more recently in Southeast Asia.[13] The construction of the 'village' includes traditional houses representing seven ethnic groups, and these are used as venues for a range of cultural activities and displays. It is officially described on the organisation's own website as a 'living museum' that 'depicts the heritage of the major racial groups in Sarawak and conveniently portrays their respective lifestyles amidst 14 acres of tropical vegetation'.[14] The vision is appropriately hyperbole as the organisation seeks to be 'a world class cultural paradise'. The Mission statement has three key aims:

1 To showcase Sarawak's multi-ethnics (sic) culture and traditions through innovative products and top-class services.
2 To give all visitors a memorable experience of Sarawak's rich cultural heritage.
3 To promote the appreciation of Sarawak's culture among the younger generation.[15]

The SCV recently celebrated 25 years of successful operations, during which it has also become the internationally well-known host of the Rainforest World Music Festival. Nevertheless, the aim to represent Sarawak's rich cultural heritage through a variety of products has also been the subject of criticism. In particular, the manner in which the representation of indigenous cultures tends to ignore the issue of authenticity has come under scrutiny. Paulette Dellios is one critic, and she has described the SCV as 'an economic similitude of a well-to-do village'.[16] As she says, 'this "mix-and-match" model of settlement patterns is entirely unrelated to kampong realities', emphasising that the danger for the conservation of cultural heritages is that the replicated village (intended in the third SCV aim, to promote the appreciation of Sarawak's culture among the younger generation) 'is drawn upon as a source of authentication'.[17]

Dellios clearly views the SCV with reference to European heritage values, where the buildings at this site are clearly not authentic because they are replicas; and, in addition, they have been assembled outside their traditional social context, appropriated for another purpose. Thus, they may be interesting but the place is essentially a theme park, devoid of truthfulness and lacking integrity. In the defence of the SCV, the non-Malay indigenous people that work in the 'village' undertake activities that are representative of longstanding arts and cultural practices, but this does not necessarily provide an example of authentic intangible culture heritage. Unfortunately, the appropriation of the idea of authentic intangible cultural heritage is also problematic. This has been argued by Graig T. Latrell, who has explored the relationship between representation and authenticity at the SCV through the lens of theatrical performance. Latrell has analysed how the experiences of the village are choreographed for ordinary tourists. He conducted fieldwork in Sarawak and Sabah supported by the Mellon Foundation in 2005 and 2006, where he researched the role of performance at the SCV and compared it with some other smaller cultural village experiences in Sabah. As a result of his analysis of visitor experiences at these places, he has described these kinds of cultural villages and shows as providing a form of '*heritainment*', which he writes is concerned with 'exhibiting authentic-seeming cultural forms while entertaining and imparting easily recalled images and narratives'.[18] Of his experience of being at the SCV, for example, he observed that:

> While the intended impression may be one of an unmediated encounter [with a range of indigenous people], it is a highly staged interaction, heightened by theatrical elements such as costumes, props, and a "living" set. The whole performance is controlled by producers in terms of casting, hours of availability and, of course, wages. While impromptu conversations with the "actors" about topics other than their heritage activities are not exactly discouraged, they tend to be limited, whether conducted in English or Bahasa Malaysia.[19]

More disturbingly perhaps, Latrell recognised that a theatrical performance known as 'the show', which utilised a cast of 48 permanent and contract performers of a range of ethnicities, was carefully orchestrated to reinforce some key themes that resonated with orthodox political rhetoric. These themes, he observed, were the diversity of Sarawak's culture, Sarawak's relation to Malaysia as a nation and Malaysia's role as an international tourist destination. While Latrell considered the first two themes problematic, particularly concerning the mythical representation of inclusion and ethnic harmony, the last provided clear evidence that the show was directly connected to the campaigns of the Malaysian Tourism Promotion Board. At the culmination of the show, Latrell was convinced that it was a 'government-devised vehicle clearly designed to elevate the national over the local'.[20] Thus performing a clever function of submerging indigenous values within a national unity narrative.

The role of the SCV in providing a means of promoting state and national government policies, in which indigenous people themselves have little agency, is to an extent mirroring the ability of indigenous people to own the representation of their cultures in mainstream society. It seems that most often indigenous communities have relied on the commercialisation of their culture through State and/or media patronage. There have therefore been legitimate questions emerging from both within indigenous organisations and from other studies concerning the agency of participants in the relationship between State patronage, heritage conservation and tourism in Sarawak. Recently, for example, researchers in Malaysia have again questioned the equitability of the benefits that may flow from the social and economic capital that is generated from tourism. They have reported that programs initiated by Tourism Malaysia and the Ministry of Culture, Arts and Tourism (MOCAT) have often lacked enough genuine participation from the indigenous rural communities that are being represented to provide any long-term benefits.[21]

Recognising the need for indigenous agency

The lack of agency in tourism and development processes is a persistent theme that is worth investigating further because it has at times given rise to ideas that have attempted to address this issue, and which in part have underpinned the motivation behind the KHCMDP. Historically, an important moment that marked the emerging voice of indigenous people concerning this and other development related issues occurred in 1999. The Dayak Cultural Foundation (DCF) convened a conference to discuss the consequences of 'a rapidly changing world' – by which they meant the impacts of globalisation and national policy – on the non-Malay indigenous cultures of Sarawak. The indigenous people of Sarawak are collectively called Dayaks, which includes the largest population group, the Iban, and close to the least populous, the Kelabit. These groups share many social and economic issues, and the meeting covered a broad range of topics, two of which are highlighted here. The first was a resolution concerning the authenticity of intangible cultural heritage such as dance and music, and stated the aim: 'That the Iban community, through the Dayak Cultural Foundation, take steps to ensure *the preservation of the authenticity* of the Iban performing arts like music and dance (ngajat)'.[22] It is difficult to say whether the direct reference to music and dance as a key part of the heritage conservation agenda was a response to the problematic admixture of representations that was occurring at the SCV, but it was nevertheless a watershed moment when the non-Malay indigenous community articulated a deep concern for the conservation and ownership of their heritages.

Additionally, at this meeting, a blueprint for the preservation and development of indigenous cultures was argued by local academic Madeline Berma. Berma suggested some very practical responses to help address the tide of changes which communities needed to address. Of high concern was the impact of rural-urban migration, a consequence of the growing dependence on cities in Sarawak for employment. This undermined the sustainability of rural villages and longhouses and in response she saw an important role for local tourism in creating employment opportunities in the affected communities.[23] However, more than that Berma recognised that if the cultures of the indigenous peoples of Sarawak were to survive, they needed to participate more effectively in the process of what was called 'cultural democracy'. At the time, this concept was being shaped by principles expounded by the then Prime Minister Dr Mahathir Mohamad in *Malaysia's Vision* 2020 and also more broadly in the development agenda he championed.[24] As Berma said,

> In Sarawak, considerable progress has been made in the last few decades in the promotion of cultural democracy, as exemplified by the state's role in organizing the Iban, Malay, Melanau, Chinese and Orang Ulu cultural seminar, the establishment of the Dayak Cultural Foundation, and sponsoring of *pua kumbu* weaving competition and exhibitions. Seminars and exhibitions alone are insufficient. The Iban communities must participate actively in negotiations with the state so that they can contribute to the formation of policies for their understanding, respect and acceptance.[25]

In Berma's view the policy of 'cultural democracy' was a national enterprise through which the Government lent backing to some authorised organisations and instigated some specific programs that contributed to its economic development goals. As Berma noted, it was either largely impervious and unresponsive to non-Malay indigenous influence or the non-indigenous Malays were lacking in the skill set to participate effectively in the political process that would help them to benefit from cultural democracy.

The ideas and strategies that were discussed at the DCF meeting in 1999 continued to resonate in the Kelabit community. The creation of innovative tourism has fuelled the creation of a constellation of supporting services in Bario. The innovative annual Food Festival established in 2005 is a major celebration of some aspects of the community's intangible cultural heritage. The community has embraced new technology and promoted the Kelabit

Highlands as a destination through a website called *eBario*, and in 2012, the first community radio station in Malaysia (*Radio Bario*) was established to promote community events. The concept of creating a museum in Bario came to be seen as a linchpin of these cultural and ecotourism projects, a destination to help orientate and shape the experiences of visitors, providing an introduction and interpretation of Kelabit values constructed by themselves. In practical terms the museum was to provide a centrally located gateway to services in the town, and a launching point for trekking to the burial sites, stone monoliths and surrounding longhouse homestays and guesthouses in the Kelabit Highlands. In recent years the tourist industry has continued to grow in Bario, with an average of three Malaysian Air Services (MAS) flights a day arriving from Miri on the north coast. Homestay businesses are now being supported by the availability of government subsidised solar generated electricity. An ever-growing number of private vehicles arrive on a four-wheel drive logging truck from Miri, which means that, at times, the town is saturated with visitors.

Presently Bario offers cultural tourism and ecotourism products created by local entrepreneurial initiative, employing local people and Indonesian guest workers. The Kelabit relationship with the land encompasses quintessential cultural heritage and natural heritage values that are being integrated into tourism products and visitor experiences. The emphasis on conservation is supported by the close proximity of the *Mulu World Heritage Area*. Additionally, other community leaders, including John Tarawe and Leila Hodder Raja (RKS committee members), have been active in campaigning for the *Heart of Borneo* conservation initiative. This is a transnational program to implement a stricter conservation framework for the island of Borneo that is supported by the World Wildlife Fund (WWF). They see ecotourism as one way in which the community might be able address the decline of the village's direct economic dependence on traditional agricultural and hunting activities. In addition, small-scale enterprises such as community initiated interpretation programs have emerged that focus on an appreciation of the unique flora and fauna and aesthetic beauty of Borneo forests. These may use traditional knowledge and promote the sustainable harvesting of food and forest products. Guides lead visitors on walking tours along established trails that link longhouses in the Kelabit Highlands, providing much needed additional income to outlying villages.

The initiatives undertaken by the RKS echo international and local models of cultural production. However, as Canadian academic Lara Hill has observed and warned, there has been a broader take-up of this strategy across many indigenous peoples, because 'cultural development has been fuelled by both the growing interest in heritage and diversity and the relevance of culture as a valuable commodity in an expanding global tourism market'.[26] While recognising this issue, the KHCMDP was underpinned by a more positive view that has been articulated by museologist Richard Sandell, that museums do have the potential to contribute to regeneration and renewal initiatives and assist a community to address its own needs.[27] Nonetheless, there were and remain many outstanding issues for this project that arise from the complex relationships between heritage conservation, representation and tourism, not least of which needed to address the question of consensus around what constitutes authentic heritage values and further, the extent to which the RKS can create social capital, trust, empathy and meaning in the community as a whole.[28] For the Kelabit community the museum may indeed bring some economic and cultural benefits. Yet there are also real needs to address the degree to which the authenticity of heritage values may be compromised by the commodification of the Kelabit Highlands and the erosion of community agency from a larger network of commercial transactions that arise from the growing integration of the Kelabit Highlands into the mainstream Malaysian tourism system. This may become a risk to the conservation of Kelabit heritage values because, as Alberto Gomes has pointed out, many indigenous communities have been increasingly marginalised 'not because they are remote *from* the centre but because they have been incorporated *by* the centre through economic and/or political means'.[29]

The political challenges are complex; however, we see participation as critical to achieving the voice of authenticity, as determined by the community. Therefore, engagement is important to help communities stay slightly out of the mainstream tourism system and maintain ownership of this project. The KHCMDP began with position that the museum would contribute to the regeneration, renewal and preservation of Kelabit cultural values, and informed by past practices, participants aimed to achieve full agency on the decisions and outward expressions regardless of the external pressures and competing interests.

Notes

1 Official Portal of Department of Orang, *Orang Asli Museum*, Department of Orang Asli Development (JAKOA), 2016, www.jakoa.gov.my/en/orang-awam/museum-of-orang-asli/, accessed 3 November 2107.
2 Iola Lenzi, *Museums of Southeast Asia*, Archipelago Press, Singapore, 2004, p. 72.
3 Jinn Winn Chong, '"Mine, Yours or Ours": The Indonesia-Malaysia Disputes over Shared Cultural Heritage', *Sojourn: Journal of Social Issues in Southeast Asia*, Vol.27, No.1, April 2012, pp. 1–53, p. 24.
4 Ibid, 2012, p. 24.
5 Ian J. Ewart, 'Social and Material Influences on the Kelabit Dwelt Environment', *TDSR*, Vol.23, No.2, 2012, pp. 69–82, p. 76.

6 Ibid, p. 81.
7 Nikki Lugun (ed), *Pesta Nukenen: Celebrating the Culture and Culinary Heritage of the Kelabit Highlands*, Rurum Kelabit Sarawak, Kuching, 2015, p. 43.
8 Ceria Group, Project Gallery, Ceria Alliance Sdn. Bhd., www.ceriagroup.org/gallery.html, accessed 21 September 2017.
9 Michelle Fine, Lois Weis, Susan Weseen and Loonmun Wong, 'For Whom? Qualitative Research, Representations, and Social Responsibilities', in Norman K. Denzin and Yvonna S. Lincoln (eds), *Handbook of Qualitative Research*, Second Edition, 2000, pp. 107–132, p. 111.
10 Nikki Lugun, 'Introduction', *Pesta Nukenen: Celebrating the Culture and Culinary Heritage of the Kelabit Highlands*, Rurum Kelabit Sarawak, Kuching, 2015, p. 9.
11 Roger W. Harris, 'Tourism in Bario, Sarawak, Malaysia: A Case Study of Pro-Poor Community-Based Tourism Integrated into Community Development', *Asia Pacific Journal of Tourism Research*, Vol.14, No.2, 2009, pp. 125–135.
12 Glenn C. Sutter, Tobias Sperlich, Douglas Worts, René Rivard and Lynne Teather, 2016, 'Fostering Cultures of Sustainability through Community-Engaged Museums: The History and Re-Emergence of Ecomuseums in Canada and the USA', *Sustainability*, Vol.8, No.1310, 2016, pp. 1–9.
13 See Michael Hitchcock, 'The Indonesian Cultural Village Museums and Its Forbears', *Journal of Museum Ethnography*, No.7, 1995, 17–24.
14 Sarawak Cultural Village, 2016, www.scv.com.my, accessed 29 May 2017.
15 Ibid, 2016.
16 Paulette Dellios, 'The Museumification of the Village: Cultural Subversion in the 21st Century', *Culture Mandala: The Bulletin of Centre for East-West Cultural and Economic Studies*, Vol.5, No.1, Article 4, 2002, p. 7, http://epublications.bond.edu.au/cm/vol5/iss1/4, accessed 3 November 2017.
17 Ibid, 2002, p. 7.
18 Craig T. Latrell, 'Exotic Dancing: Performing Tribal and Regional Identities in East Malaysia's Cultural Villages', *TDR: The Drama Review*, Vol.52, No. 4, Winter 2008, pp. 41–63. p. 42.
19 Ibid, 2008, p. 42.
20 Ibid, 2008, p. 51.
21 Puvaneswaran Kunasekaran, Sarit S. Gill, A. T. Talib, Ma'rof Redzuan, 'Culture as an Indigenous Tourism Product of Mah Meri Community in Malaysia', *Life Science Journal*, Vol.10, No. 3, 2013, pp. 1600–1604, p. 1601.
22 Dimbab Ngidang, Spencer Emading Sanggin and Robert Menua Saleh (eds), *Iban Culture and Development in the New Reality*, Dayak Cultural Foundation, Kuching, 2000, p. 114.
23 Madeline Berma, 'Beyond the 1990s: Challenges and Opportunities for the Iban', in Dimbab Ngidang, Spencer Emading Sanggin and Robert Menua Saleh (eds), *Iban Culture and Development in the New Reality*, Dayak Cultural Foundation, Kuching, 2000, pp. 76–102, p. 95.
24 Ibid, 2000, p. 100.
25 Ibid, 2000, p. 97.
26 Lara L. Hill, 'Indigenous Culture: Both Malleable and Valuable', *Journal of Cultural Heritage Management and Sustainable Development*, Vol.1, No.2, 2011, pp. 122–134, p. 124.
27 Richard Sandell, *Museums, Society, Inequality*, Routledge, London, 2002, p. 7.

28 Robert R. Janes, 'Museums, Social Responsibility and the Future', in Simon J. Knell et al. (eds), *Museum Revolutions: How Museums Change and Art Changed*, Routledge, London, 2007, p. 140.
29 Alberto Gomes, quoted in, S. Robert Aiken and Colin H. Leigh, 'Seeking Redress in the Courts: Indigenous Land Rights and Judicial Decisions in Malaysia', *Modern Asian Studies*, Vol.45, No.4, July 2010, pp. 825–875, p. 841.

5 Indigenous knowledge in community museum practice

Introduction

As a legacy of the colonial period, the Federal Constitution in Malaysian law defines the Kelabit people as 'natives' and has implications for their access to 'Native Customary Land' and other matters.[1] While their status as an entity in law is obviously critical, in considering the relationships between community and identity, and heritage conservation and cultural representation that are central to this book, we are faced with a greater complexity because of the community's experiences since WWII. For this reason, we have hypothesised that it is useful to situate the analysis of the conceptualisation and activities of the KHCMDP in an entrepreneurial development space. Additionally, 'new museology' recognises the problematic cultural construction of terms such as 'western museum' and 'non-western museum', and also fosters the relevance of different knowledge systems.

It is tempting perhaps to describe the RKS initiative as the creation of an 'indigenous museum', but as Christina Kreps has suggested of similar projects, this has limited value beyond being a convenient interpretive means of identifying and analysing the similarities and differences that it may have with other museums in national and other cultural contexts.[2] Nevertheless, the designation of the Kelabit as indigenous people of Borneo has circumscribed their status, and this has certainly informed the conceptualisation of the museum. From the start, the RKS was interested in using the museum as a vehicle for conserving selected cultural values, as well as aspiring to harness heritage resources that were appropriated by others in the colonial past, reflecting a contemporary approach to heritage conservation and cultural representation which utilises a modern communication framework that draws upon the history of museums.

Community museum: a form of representation

The process of heritage selection is unique and very complex, and is mediated by the community's experiences of religion and education since WWII.

In the main, the Kelabit people practice the Christian faith very seriously and their beliefs have contributed to a new process of identity construction and a cohesiveness that has shaped their current views on the purposes of culture and heritage. This process is further nuanced through the participation of Kelabit people in mainstream Malaysian society over the past two generations. Most important is those community-minded individuals who are orchestrating the KHCMDP through the RKS have achieved positions of professional influence across many aspects of Malaysian society, including academia, business, politics, law and medicine. This is significant because in addressing key development goals there is a high level of professional capacity available to the community. These people are motivated and well placed to try to facilitate access to educational, governmental and financial resources that are utilised to enhance the resilience of Kelabit culture.

Rather than describe the project as an indigenous museum development, which implies an unrealistic dichotomy between indigenous values and contemporary processes of conservation and representation, the term 'community museum' was adopted by the project very early on.[3] This recognised the broad use of the term in many other jurisdictions, and acknowledges that many people have organised themselves into 'museum communities' that may represent ethnic and religious identity or particular interests, such as historical, social and technological themes.[4] In 2010 Francesco Bandarin of UNESCO wrote that 'this process is part of the creation of an imagined, though not wholly subjective, sense of a common destiny among the peoples concerned'.[5] The designation of the project as a 'community museum' project reflected this intent but also recognised a broader sphere in which these aims and ambitions are shared by other communities who are not necessarily concerned with indigenous issues. It was also expedient because it allowed for a breadth of creativity that encompassed the possibility of an entrepreneurial development process in which cultural representation was addressed strategically and necessarily outside the State museum system.

As a type, the distinguishing feature of community museums is that they are grounded in the actions of communities rather than established by governments. It is worth saying that these have been referred to in a number of ways, depending on the context in which they have been operating; as indigenous museums, ecomuseums or community museums. Although there are obvious variables from one to another, in general these types of museums coalesce around a vision of inclusiveness and often share the following foundation principles. Firstly, the museum aims to be a means in which the represented community have a high degree of agency in the interpretation of their culture and heritage. Secondly, this is achieved through the participation of members of the community; and thirdly, the museum seeks to contribute to the resilience and sustainability of the community through facilitating engagement with significant contemporary issues. As Jonathan Sweet and Jo Wills have observed 'many inclusive forms of museum practice that integrate development principles, occur at the local level because they are not as entrenched in institutional hierarchy as larger, more traditional museums'.[6]

A process of representation is embedded within the concept of the ecomuseum, where a sense of place, including 'landscape, buildings, ways of life, material culture in all its forms, traditions and much more' becomes the link between the community and the public.[7] As an alternative to the traditional European collection based museum, which separates people from objects, the philosophy of the ecomuseum recognises the integration of people and environment, nature and culture, and as a potential form of conservation and representation it has attracted much attention. Artur Hazelius (1833–1933) first advanced the concept of the ecomuseum[8] as a concept in which local distinctions form the spirit of the place and develop a strong sense of local pride in traditions and customs. Ecomuseums need to be products of their own community, developed and managed by the community, and they must act as the safeguard and site of representation for the community's living heritage, addressing local issues and presenting a shared vision for the area.[9] It is therefore essential that the governance of the museum resides within the community itself, and there is also a focus on the creation of a place for self-knowledge, learning and the practicing of skills. A successful ecomuseum can also be a critical asset as a location for community problem solving. Thus, with clear objectives and a policy framework, this model of conservation can act as a form of community engagement with an emphasis on sustainable community development.[10]

Although the principle idea of Hazelius was to restore villages to preserve rural areas, the concept of the ecomuseum has evolved to include the preservation of natural ecosystems in conjunction with the development of conventional museums. George Henri Riveire (1987–1985) redefined the idea of the ecomuseum as one which recognises the synergy between history and progress and the social and natural surrounds of a community, and argued that it should facilitate the social development of the community.[11] The objectives of the KHCMDP align very closely with the ambition of Riviere's conception where the intention was to create a place which would foster the local history, heritage values and contemporary culture of the Kelabit people, and in turn be a place to debate and represent a possible future for a community, while also providing an economic and tourist opportunity. It is worth emphasising that ecomuseums tend to stand independent of political affiliations, and as discussed earlier, the Kelabit community is undertaking this project independently. Under these circumstances, the community museum may potentially fill the void left by the changing role of the Bario Asal. As yet the scope of the cultural remit of the organisation is not well defined, especially because of the difficulties of negotiating and articulating heritage values in a fragile hybrid culture.

The challenge of articulating cultural heritage values

The process of defining heritage values within a community is seldom straightforward and without contestation. In this case where the process needs to be inclusive of a small but dispersed membership, there are a range of issues. A key issue in the project was gaining access to reliable information that could support an argument for articulating significant heritage values, based on the concept of authenticity. Whilst key aspects of intangible heritage, such as cuisine and performance, may have to some extent survived through continuous practice in longhouses, much of the traditional knowledge and other 'stories' that have survived from life before WWII are based on the memories of the elderly, who are declining in numbers. Critically, the memories (and other abilities) of these elders are often compromised by poor health. Where in the past opportunities for sharing this knowledge with the younger members of the community were integrated into longhouse life, the movement of younger people to education and employment outside the community has ruptured the lines of transmission and hindered the passing of knowledge from one generation to another. Currently few children born in the last twenty years speak the Kelabit language, and many know very little about the life of their ancestors before WWII. Where stories and songs have been transcribed and published, these books are rarely available in the Highlands, underlining the need for the museum to also act as a repository of resources.

This is particularly important because the traditional processes that facilitated the transmission of knowledge were fixed in social practices that were critical to the maintenance of cohesion in longhouses. As the Kelabit came into contact with Europeans, this process of transmission was increasingly eroded. Additionally, although the documentation of Kelabit culture was increasingly undertaken or facilitated by researchers from outside the community, the motivation for undertaking this research was different and the effectiveness of this research was limited. In the nineteenth century, some aspects of the life of the Kelabit were described by colonial administrative officials or their associates. Nevertheless, these are especially rare because unlike other tribes in Sarawak, the Kelabit people had little contact with the Brooke administration and the outside world until WWII. An influential exception was District officer Charles Hose, who is best known for his account of indigenous people in *The Pagan Tribes of Borneo*, 1912, and the later book *Natural Man. A Record from Borneo*, 1924, which was a 'selectively extracted and revised' version of the earlier book designed for wider consumption.¹² As a resident in Barum between 1891 and 1904, he was well situated to undertake fieldwork, and in the process, he also formed a substantial collection of artefacts, much of which is preserved at the University of Cambridge.

In the first decade of the twentieth century, Hose assiduously documented the body adornment of the people in the Highlands in collaboration with the Sarawak Museum curator Robert Shelford. An article they published in 1906 reported this research and included illustrations of a distinct range of Kelabit tattoo designs.¹³ Although this kind of scholarly documentation is rare, the article seems to provide a reliable source of information concerning the cultural tradition in which women in particular where heavily tattooed as a symbol of strength. Older women bearing these tattoos are currently evident in Bario, but the tradition is no longer practiced. We may accept that these illustrations were accurate representations of Kelabit designs, but it is nevertheless important to appreciate, as Hose scholar Brian Durrans has argued, that colonial administrators and collectors were actors within a colonial system, and accordingly the work of Hose and Shelford is an example of how knowledge about the indigenous peoples of Borneo was selectively constructed according to a particular mindset during the rule of the White Rajas; thus the motivations and the outcomes of the process need to be treated with some circumspection.¹⁴ During the period of decolonisation after WWII, the international interest in the exotic and unknown Kelabit people grew, particularly through the work of Harrisson. His autobiographical account of wartime experiences in the book *World Within* also provided descriptions of many activities undertaken by the inhabitants of Bario Asal.¹⁵ Snapshots of life in this longhouse were documented by the photographer Hetta Morrison, who gained privileged access in the 1950s. These detailed black and white photographs are included in the book *Sarawak* that was published in 1957.¹⁶

Perhaps the most significant example of sustained academic research into the traditions and practices of the Kelabit is that conducted by the British anthropologist Monica Janowski. Janowski is unique for the maintenance of a very longstanding personal relationship with the Kelabit community over many decades. Initially she conducted extensive fieldwork in Sarawak and lived with the community in the Kelabit Highlands while completing her Doctorate, which was submitted in 1991. It was titled *Rice, Work and Community Among the Kelabit of Sarawak, East Malaysia*. This work drew not only upon written accounts of the history of the Kelabit by their own people but also on oral accounts provided by members of the community at that time. It documented and proportioned significance to key aspects of Kelabit culture and society, and remains a key foundation work of anthropological scholarship for this subject. However, as Janowski demonstrated, 30 years ago the information that was contributed by members of the community about their history and the structure of traditional society before WWII was at times ambiguous, especially when it came to specific details. For example, the discussion concerning leadership in which there was some consensus in the Kelabit accounts that there existed four classes, but disagreement about what these classes consisted of. Upon further investigation, including linguistic analysis, Janowski concluded that while there may have been a basic class structure, 'there are nowadays and probably were in the past no individuals or hearth-groups which have any rights that other individuals or hearth-groups do not have', and furthermore that the concept of 'prestige' which a class structure embodies 'for the Kelabit, derives from the taking of responsibility for others'.[17] In one respect this observation makes sense in accounting for the motivation of the members of the RKS to assist with the conservation of Kelabit culture and promote community interests. Nevertheless, this kind of analysis also highlights a problem in the process of heritage-making during the project because it underscores the complexity and difficulties that researchers both from within and from outside the community have faced in trying to ascertain what may constitute traditional Kelabit values.

In seeking to understand the spiritual values of Kelabit culture, Janowski made an audio recording of a live telling of the epic Kelabit story known as the 'Legend of Tuked Rini'. Janowski describes Tuked Rini, whose stellar deeds figure in this myth, as the equivalent of a cultural hero, someone who established fundamental laws about the way that people should live; he is regarded as the ancestor of all the people of the Kelapang River area. On this occasion, an oration by the tribal elder Balang Pelaba took place at Pa'Dalih in 1986, and it was attended by many of the inhabitants of the longhouse. It was the first telling of this epic for many years and was perhaps one of only three times that this important story had been told since the 1940s.[18] The version of the story told by Balang Pelaba took one and a half hours to complete, and of this kind of oral performance Janowski wrote:

> It is clear that while there is a core structure to the Legend, there are many different versions and many different possible episodes, each focusing on a particular head hunting expedition. Each teller seems to favour different episodes and it is almost certain that each time the Legend is told the teller changes it.[19]

As there is no authoritative written text, and there are few people with detailed knowledge of the story, the selectivity and personality of the teller is evident in its performance. Consequently, fixing one authoritative version or even a range of versions is a difficult task. Storytellers are free to interpret this important foundation myth as they think seems fit.

Indigenous knowledge 63

The limited availability of authoritative historical sources, records of traditional stories and knowledge, are not unique to the Kelabit people, and they share similar issues with other indigenous peoples who have strong oral traditions through which heritage values maintain currency, but which have been compromised by significant change to the structure and fabric of the society. This is an important issue for the process of heritage construction because to arrive at any consensus, members of the community are challenged by the complexities of having to navigate, negotiate and distil key values from the current memories of members of the community or from those stories documented in recent decades, which may not be understood or shared.

Creating agency in cultural heritage development

Diversity within distinct communities means the extent to which the membership is said to have agency in the process of heritage conservation and cultural representation and the extent to which there is broad inclusion are important questions. Research into community museums in various contexts has drawn attention to variables such as the nature of leadership and governance, the kinds of heritage assets that are available to the museum and the purposes for which educational or interpretative programs are envisaged and prioritised. In a comparative study of ecomuseums in Japan published in 2004, Peter Davis observed that the democratisation (the extent of inclusiveness) of these projects was in part contingent on the efforts of the leadership.[20] This was of some relevance in thinking about the methodology applied in KHCMDP: the RKS leadership clearly saw their role as one of facilitating the development process and of seeking to build support for the project through strategically facilitated community consultation. As this account will relate, this was artfully pursued through respecting traditional systems of longhouse governance and utilising contemporary urban and social media networks.

Additionally, in conceptualising a vision for the project, there was a need to consider the question of what would make a community museum a successful enterprise. In this the work of the anthropologist and museologist Christina Kreps was very useful because it had currency gained from her research into indigenous curatorship and traditional methods of conservation, and her aligned knowledge and experience of similar community enterprises in Southeast Asia.[21] Kreps articulated two clear criteria in 2007 that resonated with the ambitions of the KHCMDP:

> For community-based museums success might rest on the degree to which they are fully integrated into a community's cultural life and help sustain and conserve its cultural traditions, as well as what they

contribute to the socioeconomic development of the community, its sense of place and identity.[22]

In aspirational terms, this was useful for focusing the goals of the KHCMDP because it is broadly conceived and inclusive enough to accommodate a range of operational models. This was attractive because as the project matures, the community will necessarily negotiate ideas, heritage assets and the challenges of integrating community values, interests and capabilities into the life of the museum. This means that the Kelabit have scope for innovation and may develop and administer their museum and cultural centre as they see fit. Furthermore, while assessing the successfulness of the project at this point may be difficult, the criteria recognised that the contemporary circumstances of such community-based projects may create circumstances in which the community has agency in fostering innovative forms of conservation that may arise from the melding of traditional cultural practices and development processes.

Consequently, this research relies on the concepts of collective community agency for the project to be sustainable. Types of agency can include human, individual, collective, intentional and conscious.[23] Laura Ahearn takes the position that agency is defined as the 'socioculturally mediated capacity to act' but acknowledges this definition is open to interpretation, leaving many details unspecified.[24] She identifies the ability of creating empowerment through linguistic exchange using words and texts that are socially and geographically situated and uses the example of place making through storytelling to examine how understanding and meaning are assembled, serving to shape future conduct and the social construct. These notions of agency are strongly aligned with the KHCMDP, and as Jane Hill and Judith Irvine explain:

> interpreting events, establishing facts, conveying opinion, and constituting interpretations as knowledge are all activities involving socially situated participants, who are agents in the construction of knowledge and agents when they act on what they have come to know, believe, suspect, or opine.[25]

Ahearn also recognises agency is strongly associated with action theories, as agency requires a sense of commitment to an intent. In other words, concepts of agency have implications for action and the intentions of human nature. Yet the KHCMDP occurs as a collective community activity. Jean Lave and Etienne Wenger use the term 'community of practice' to define a group of people who come together around an agreed endeavour.[26] Seen as different from a traditional construct of community, a community of practice is defined by a sense of purpose and by the practice in which that community shares mutual engagement. Individuals commonly participate in multiple membership that may constrain or enable agency. Translating this into the process of the KHCMDP, we can say that essentially two communities of practice converged; the Kelabit community and the Deakin University community. Furthermore, in terms of actions, the Kelabit community directed the outcomes of the project, while the consultant DU team acted as facilitators in a decision-making process.

Relatively recently, UNESCO and its affiliated organisation ICCROM have strongly advocated for the codification of participatory approaches to conservation, designed to recognise and enhance the agency of local communities. Particularly relevant was the process of creating the 2005 *Hoi An Protocols For Best Conservation Practice in Asia: Professional Guidelines For Assuring and Preserving the Authenticity of Heritage Sites in the Context of the Cultures of Asia*. Here, heritage professionals from a range of countries, including Paiman Bin Keromo, General Director, Department of Museums and Antiquities Malaysia, were motivated by the essential interwoven connections between tangible and intangible expressions of historical, social and religious values that often define communities in Southeast Asia. *The Hoi An Protocols* aimed to address a key threat to heritage conservation, stating that 'the greatest danger to longer-term safeguarding of the heritage of Asia . . . is inadequate public understanding of the need to conserve heritage and inadequate localization of stewardship responsibility over heritage resources'.[27] These were astute observations based on widespread and deep understandings of heritage conservation in Asia by UNESCO personnel and State representatives. The subsequent advocacy for the recognition and enhancement of local stewardship and responsibility for heritage resources was particularly relevant to the conceptualisation of KHCMDP.

The Hoi An Protocols for Best Conservation Practice in Asia responded to the threat of increased globalisation, the loss of traditional knowledge among younger generations and the need to map the diversity of intangible forms of knowledge to support preservation efforts.[28] It also focused on the pressure of tourism to commodify cultural assets, which leads to standardisation and loss of authenticity in the replication of cultural forms. The *Hoi An Protocols* identified cultural heritage as a knowledge resource, and to safeguard authenticity, recommended an assessment of the carrying capacity of the site, the design and enforcement of defensive regulations to protect heritage, the need for planning to manage processes of change and creative financing and incentive mechanisms to aid conservation. Echoing the theory of community and ecomuseums, the document clearly stated that 'ultimately, the idea of cultural heritage is rooted in a sense of place and a sense of self-identity and public education, on-site education needs to be adapted to the needs of the Asian context'.[29] Each of these aims were reflected in the KHCMDP process, where there was a need to address the younger generations who are not connecting with traditional knowledge and where the commodification of cultural assets impacts on the authenticity of representation.

Thus, more recently, museology has incorporated critical perspectives concerning the roles and functions museums have in shaping societies across a broad spectrum. More particularly, in some sectors heritage practitioners and academics have also advocated the recognition and incorporation of local indigenous knowledge systems and traditions in the processes of conservation, addressing the perceived dominance of western methodologies.[30] This, they believe, has increasingly become critical to the survival of the cultures of poorly resourced indigenous peoples. In part, this is symbolised by the urgency in which a discourse addressing the concept of 'cultural landscapes' has been pursued in archaeological and heritage circles in recent years. In this discussion, it is asserted that cultural and environment conservation are closely connected.

Ngidang has described how the indigenous people of Sarawak see the relationship with land ownership in terms of a spiritual significance connected to their traditional belief systems.[31] This is intertwined with subsistence farming practices, where land is a resource for continuing sustenance and livelihood. In Ngidang's own words, the land is a 'lifeline' and 'apart from their own labour, land is the only resource that longhouse people have'. This concept has also influenced the parameters in which the KHCMDP needs to be understood as a representation of a broader set of Kelabit cultural and spiritual values. In some cases, this is reflective of the deep connections the Kelabit people maintain with the ancient and largely pristine environment in central Borneo in which people have lived for hundreds of years, as demonstrated by recent archaeological projects, and the cultural agrarian and hunting practices that are profoundly connected to it. For the Kelabit this project not only incorporates a heartfelt concern for the survival of their own culture, but it also necessitates a pragmatic engagement with government planning and native land rights issues, which they perceive have a range of consequences for the conservation of greater Borneo.

There is therefore a question concerning the ways in which knowledge is defined, and in the context of Sarawak in the past 30 years, one of the ways in which indigenous knowledge has been conceptualised is through its connection to environmental issues. This was clearly a powerful presence in the Kelabit Highlands during the project and challenged the ways in which indigenous knowledge was discussed. J. Peter Brosius, some years ago, made the point that the notion of indigenous knowledge in Sarawak, especially for those remote tribes such as the Penan whose culture and livelihood were inextricably bound to forests threatened by logging, was profoundly linked to broader environmental issues by western scientific researchers and environmental activists. Brosius believes that these people engaged in 'valorizing strategies', which require 'the deployment of a discourse that places indigenous knowledge at its center'. This narrative links indigenous knowledge to the preservation of biodiversity, and also seeks to transform 'knowledge' into 'wisdom'.[32] His analysis of the ways in which the Penan have been the focus of valorising discourse raised some important questions about the relationships between conservation and indigenous knowledge, and the associated case of the Kelabit interest in a heritage-making process. As Brosius reiterated recently (worth quoting in full):

> I have attempted to show how, in effect to make a people narratable and to create value (all while essentializing them as "forest people"), environmentalist discourse about indigenous knowledge has the potential to transform that knowledge into something it is not. To save something, or to mobilize an audience to want to save something, requires that it be made beautiful or profound or have some transcendent value. In creating that value, however, the thing is transformed. Thus, the rich, if generally mundane, Penan knowledge of the forest landscape, by being transformed into something that is sacred, valued, and thus saved, is constructed in terms and categories that are western in origin. We see here a hall of mirrors of representation – simulacra – as Penan knowledge is transformed into something that it is not, and Western discourses are transported to Penan, who again convey them to Western interlocutors.[33]

Taking this on board, the Kelabit Highlands Community Museum was seen as an opportunity to provide the platform for a high degree of ownership in the interpretation of Kelabit indigenous knowledge and its interwoven relationship with the environment. It was seen to offer the perfect opportunity for contemporary concerns to be articulated and displayed, developing a means of galvanising the community by facilitating engagement with significant contemporary issues. The museum would be the place where the necessity for the conservation of greater Borneo can be articulated in the context of its impact on the survival of the Kelabit culture. For this reason, the KHCMDP found its way to become critical for the preservation of Kelabit cultural life, the sustainability of cultural traditions, a means for economic development and a way of creating a focus on contemporary concerns impacting the Highlands and surrounding regions.

Notes

1 Ramy Bulan, 'Boundaries, Territorial Domains, and Kelabit Customary Practices: Discovering the Hidden Landscape', *Borneo Research Bulletin*, Vol.34, 2003, pp.18–61, p. 51.
2 Christina Kreps, 'The Theoretical Future of Indigenous Museums', in Nick Stanley (ed), *The Future of Indigenous Museums: Perspectives from the Southwest Pacific*, Berghahn Books, New York and Oxford, 2007, pp. 223–234, p. 225.
3 N. Stanley, *The Future of Indigenous Museums: Perspectives from the Southwest Pacific*, Berghahn Books, New York and Oxford, 2007.
4 For example, see, N.H. Denis (ed), *Community-Based Approach to Museum Development in Asia and the Pacific for Culture and Sustainable Development*, UNESCO, Paris, 2010.
5 Francesco Bandarin, 'Preface', in Nao Hayashi Denis (ed), *Community-Based Approach to Museum Development in Asia and the Pacific for Culture and Sustainable Development*, UNESCO, Paris, 2010, pp. 4–9, p. 4.
6 Jonathan Sweet and Jo Wills, 'Cultural Heritage and Development in South East Asia', in Matthew Clarke (ed), *Handbook of Research on Development and Religion*, Edward Elgar, Cheltenham, 2013, pp. 338–355, p. 342.
7 Peter Davis, *Ecomuseums – A Sense of Place*, Second Edition, Continuum, London, 2010, p. 238.
8 L. Jeong-Hwan, Y. Won-Keun, C. Sik-In and K. Jin-Hyuk, 'Conservation of Korean Rural Heritage through the use of Ecomuseums', *Journal of Resources & Ecology*, Vol.7, No.3, 2016, pp. 163–169, p. 164.
9 Glenn C. Sutter, Tobias Sperlich, Douglas Worts, René Rivard and Lynne Teather, 'Fostering Cultures of Sustainability through Community-Engaged Museums: The History and Re-Emergence of Ecomuseums in Canada and the USA', *Sustainability*, Vol.8, No.1310, 2016, pp. 1–9, p. 4.
10 Ibid, 2016, p. 2.
11 L. Jeong-Hwan, Y. Won-Keun, C. Sik-In and K. Jin-Hyuk, 'Conservation of Korean Rural Heritage through the Use of Ecomuseums', *Journal of Resources & Ecology*, Vol.7, No.3, 2016, pp. 163–169, p. 164.
12 Brian Durrans, 'Introduction', in Charles Hose (ed), *Natural Man a Record from Borneo*, Oxford University Press, Singapore, Oxford and New York, 1988, p. vii–xv, p. xii.
13 Charles Hose and R. Shelford, 'Materials for the Study of Tatu in Borneo', *The Journal of the Anthropological Institute of Great Britain and Ireland*, January–June 1906, pp. 79–80, Plate XII, Figs.1–4, (ix+60–91).
14 Brian Durrans, 'Introduction', in Charles Hose (ed), *Natural Man a Record from Borneo*, Oxford University Press, Singapore, Oxford and New York, 1988, p. vii–xv, p. xii.
15 Tom Harrisson, *World Within: A Borneo Story*, The Cresset Press, London, 1959.
16 Hedda Morrison, *Sarawak*, MacGibbon & Kee, London, 1957.
17 Monika Janowski, *Rice, Work and Community Among the Kelabit of Sarawak, East Malaysia*, PhD thesis, London School of Economics, University of London, 1991, p. 186, p. 193.
18 Monica Janowski, *Tuked Rini, Cosmic Traveller: Life and Legend in the Heart Borneo*, Nordic Institute of Asian Studies Monograph Series, No.125, 2014,

pp. 10–11, p. 8. 'Tuki Rini is regarded as a common ancestor of all the people of the Kelapang River area, although there is no genealogy linking him directly to anyone living. He is a "culture hero" – someone who establishes fundamental rules about the way in which people should live.'
19 Ibid, 2014, p. 10.
20 Peter Davis, 'Ecomuseums and the Democratisation of Japanese Museology', *International Journal of Heritage Studies*, Vol.10, No.1, 2004, pp. 93–110, p. 93.
21 See Christina Kreps, *Liberating Culture: Cross-Cultural Perspectives on Museums, Curation and Heritage Preservation*, Routledge, London, 2003. And, Christina Kreps, 'Indigenous Curation, Museums and Intangible Cultural Heritage', in Laurajane Smith and Natsuko Akagawa (eds), *Intangible Heritage*, Routledge, London, 2009, pp. 193–208.
22 Christina Kreps, 'The Theoretical Future of Indigenous Museums', in Nick Stanley (ed), *The Future of Indigenous Museums: Perspectives from the Southwest Pacific*, Berghahn Books, New York and Oxford, 2007, pp. 223–234, p. 225.
23 Laura M. Ahearn, 'Language and Agency', *Annual Review of Anthropology*, Vol.109, 2001, pp. 109–137, p. 130.
24 Ibid, 2001, p. 112.
25 Jane H Hill and Judith T Irvine, *Responsibility and Evidence in Oral Discourse*, Cambridge University Press, Cambridge and New York, 1993, p. 2.
26 Jean Lave and Etienne Wenger, *Situated Learning: Legitimate Peripheral Participation*, Cambridge University Press, Cambridge and New York, 1991.
27 Richard A. Engelhardt and Pamela Rumball Rogers, *Hoi An Protocols for Best Conservation Practice in Asia: Professional Guidelines for Assuring and Preserving the Authenticity of Heritage Sites in the Context of the Cultures of Asia*, UNESCO, Asia and Pacific Regional Bureau for Education, Bangkok, 2009, p. 3.
28 Ibid, 2009.
29 Ibid, 2009, p. 15.
30 Christina K. Kreps, *Liberating Culture: Cross-Cultural Perspectives on Museums, Curation and Heritage Preservation*, Routledge, London, 2003.
31 Dimbab Ngidang, Spencer Emading Sanggin and Robert Menua Saleh (eds), *Iban Culture and Development in the New Reality*, Dayak Cultural Foundation, Kuching, 2000.
32 J. Peter Brosius, 'Endangered Forest, Endangered People: Environmentalist Representations of Indigenous Knowledge', in Nora Haenn, Richard R. Wilk and Alllison Harnish (eds), *The Environment in Anthropology*, Second Edition, New York University Press, New York, 2016, pp. 254–273, p. 259.
33 Ibid, p. 268.

6 Shaping the discussion on conservation

Introduction

The museum development project tells a story of the circumstances and processes through which the Kelabit are negotiating and employing the conditions of modernity, nationalism and globalisation; and, through this process, seeking to assert greater cultural agency in the conservation of heritage values and representation of their culture. The RKS decisions that were made along the way can be located within a matrix of influential personal, historical and cultural relationships which have influenced the results, including the realisation of a handsome vernacular museum building completed in 2016. In view of this, the book contributes to our understanding of the ways in which small communities in Southeast Asia are engaging with their cultural heritage through weighing up the relationships between international modern approaches to conservation and local traditional knowledge, practices and experiences, especially concerning the strategies for defining and asserting their identity more clearly. These aspirations influenced and framed how the community pursued the process of representation and navigated the relationships between the authenticity of heritage values and their interpretation.

This chapter will therefore focus on the personal perspectives of the Kelabit, locating the experiences of members of the community within an historical, social and political context that foregrounds the relationships between the role of Christianity, western education and post-colonial development issues such as the contestation over natural resources. These experiences and debates have impacted on the lives of the Kelabit and challenged their own understanding of how they have evolved since WWII. This chapter also recognises that driving the KHCMDP was a whole community process of discovery, fuelling the desire to articulate key Kelabit heritage values worth celebrating and conserving.

Awakening of heritage preservation

Dato Isaac Lugun was the President of RKS during much of the time of the KHCMDP, and he was responsible for leading the KHCMDP during this critical period in which the museum building was completed. Lugun is a lawyer and businessman based in Kuching who, like other members of the executive committee, maintains a strong connection to his home village in the Kelabit Highlands. As a parent, Lugun has pondered the question of what, if anything, do his own children know of their Kelabit roots; and, he and his wife Nikki Lugun, a photographer and writer, have sought to engage with, articulate and promote aspects of Kelabit culture. In 2012, Dato Isaac Lugun said in a formal interview that one of the key reasons the RKS was interested in exploring the idea of founding a museum was as a means to help address the concern within the community surrounding the key question of identity; 'exactly what', he asked, 'does it mean to be a Kelabit?'[1]

This reflected a deeply held feeling that the community was losing a sense of the traditional Kelabit values that were critical to its identity. This dissolution had been occurring over three generations, with Lugun belonging to the second of these. Going back to the decolonisation of Sarawak after WWII, it is interesting that the potential for this kind of loss or diminishing sense of identity was something Tom Harrisson pondered, particularly after the creation of the nation state of Malaysia.

> In Sarawak, although there are only quite small numbers of people like Kelabits, they nevertheless are very strongly Kelabits. Even if they are cutting their hair, or going to school, or being Christians (which they are increasingly), or possibly later on becoming Mohammedans, the strength of their tribal identification is likely not only to remain, but possibly to increase. This is, of course, not necessarily unhealthy or contradictory within Malaysia, because these people have got to have a very strong feeling of identification, especially when they are being asked to suffer considerably under the Confrontation.[2]

It is worth noting that Harrisson expressed his opinion during the most stressful period of Kelabit experience after WWII, sparked by the additional trauma of the Confrontation with Indonesia (1962–1966), during which many Kelabit people were relocated from outlying villages. Even while these people faced a range of pressures from a raft of political and social changes, there was something about the ingrained strength of Kelabit identity that would ensure its survival.

The Kelabit intellectuals pursuing this heritage-making project were not naive to the social role of museums or the conservation and research aims of the curators, anthropologists and archaeologists. They were the beneficiaries of quality education established during the British colonial period after WWII (1946–1963), and indeed, some older members of this group who grew up in the Bario Asal had personal contact with Harrisson, which has been described to the authors as almost familial. This was critical to the awakening of heritage consciousness in the 1960s and represented something of a counterpoint to the influence of Christianity. As a member of the British colonial administration of Sarawak, Harrisson was associated with an empirical paradigm that was profoundly influential, and during the post-war years of decolonisation, members of the RKS started to encounter western classroom-based education. It is therefore useful to provide some historical background to the changes in education policy and programs that were introduced by the British. To begin with, the colonial government had pursued a proactive approach to the education of indigenous people that was in contrast to the Brookes' administration. Ooi Keat Gin argued, for example, that White Rajas maintained a 'paternalistic approach . . . in wanting to preserve the cultural and racial integrity of the native races' and thus they offered little in the way of education and schools, particularly for rural indigenous people.[3] In contrast, the colonial government's focus (designed before it became clear that Sarawak would join the Malaysian Federation) was on achieving two main objectives: The first was to prepare the colony for self-government, ensuring the inclusion of the non-Malay indigenous people in the administration, and the second was to create an education policy which aimed 'to develop among the multi-ethnic younger generation a sense of common citizenship, identity, brotherhood and undivided loyalty to Sarawak'.[4] From the perspective of the colonial government, the need for expanding the access indigenous people had to western-style education was self-evident, and also underscored by an estimate made in a 1937 report that only 642 indigenous people (across all groups) attended school, and by another survey from the Population Census of 1947 that the illiteracy rates of indigenous peoples were between 93% and 98%.[5]

Local Authority schools were established and supported during this period, and to some extent these eroded the influence of the Christian mission schools, which were encouraged to reposition themselves as partners within the broader education system. The subsequent growth in student attendance was in part the result of direct government funding and the provision of grants, which provided rural schools with a range of resources that included school buildings, furniture and equipment, teachers' quarters and student boarding facilities. The resourcing was also accompanied by the levying of very low school fees, which 'encouraged the poorer indigenous peoples to send their children to school without undue financial burden on the family'.[6] Nevertheless, in most rural schools there were still numerous problems, such as a shortage of trained teachers (to some extent alleviated by the Colombo Plan, which bought teachers from Australia, New Zealand or Canada)[7] and also the provision of boarding subsidies and scholarships, which provided for native children to attend schools in regional centres. Of these years, Ooi Keat Gin argued, the attitudes of natives towards this expansion of education was generally favourable, instigating a '"rush" for education' that 'was contagious' and drew in 'isolated tribes like the Kelabits'.[8] There was a steady growth in the number of indigenous children attending schools during the 1950s; and in 1961, the Sarawak Information Service claimed that there were 57,700 native students attending schools.[9] Thus by the time that Sarawak joined the Malaysian Federation in 1963 and even during the years of the Confrontation that lingered on afterwards, Kelabit children were beginning to have access to western-style education.

The blending of influences, Christian spirituality, western epistemology and the continuity of longhouse village communities in which Kelabit stories were shared between generations began to affect how young Kelabit people understood their identity and heritage. The genesis of this process is expressed here in the words of the RKS Council Member and former Bario secondary school principal, Lucy Bulan:

> I remember in the sixties when we started going to school, when almost everything was gone, that we discovered that even our dances were no longer being practiced, and then we started saying "surely not everything Kelabit is wrong, it cannot be that everything western is right, it cannot be that everything western is Christian and everything Kelabit is non-Christian, *it cannot be, there must be something in our culture that surely can be considered still good, not un-Christian*, in particular". So, very consciously, we brought back the dances, which we had thrown away, and there were discussions, I remember, about what are the things that we could still keep doing and what are the sorts of things we must not do anymore. . . .[10]

Bulan's reflection on the experiences of her generation recognises that they were initiating a heritage-making process which was pursued within a context of cultural hybridity and political uncertainty. This needed to grapple with and locate the relative significance of distinct and convergent aspects of Kelabit memory, experiences and knowledge. The choice of exploring dance may have been a non-controversial strategy that had the potential to galvanise the community and, in the event, it had important consequences. These dances are now a feature of Kelabit cultural life in Bario and are regularly performed by a range of local women and men. Additionally, these performances have also necessitated proficiencies in a range of associated activities, such as costume design and making, the singing of stories and the use of traditional musical instruments. This has also spurred on the creation of contemporary music that draws on traditional sources to create something new.

It is clear that the effects of change over the past half-century have concerned many Kelabit people, and through their engagement with higher education some members of the community have undertaken historical, anthropological and sociological research into their own circumstances, with a view to understanding how western culture has influenced the values and circumstances of contemporary Kelabit society. In this respect, Dato Isaac Lugun and Lucy Bulun are not the only ones to apply their professional expertise to the question of identity. Dr Poline Bala is another member of the RKS executive committee, and an academic at the University of Malaysia, Sarawak (UNIMAS). Bala has researched the question of identity, particularly focused on the relationship between Christian doctrine, traditional Kelabit values and modernity. These have a complex and emotive relationship, and she has written about how the impact of Christianity in the 1950s had 'a contradictory, double role among the Kelabit'; in part, disconnecting the past and affirming some Kelabit practices, which provided a conceptual bridge to the Malaysian government's political goals of modernity and progress after 1963.[11] For example, Bala has argued that the traditional Kelabit value of achievement meant that some Kelabit people were able to prosper through the opportunities offered by modernity.

The questions raised by the Luguns, Bala and Bulan are examples of the concern and strategies through which the Kelabit leadership have pursued the questions of heritage-making and identity. Nevertheless, the issue of negotiating the distinctions between history and heritage and confronting the potential difficulties of heritage interpretation are matters that may require much more attention from the community, particularly if there is a serious intent to distil Kelabit values for the benefit of visitors and more importantly for social development, particularly to engage and benefit the next generation.

Contestation and the cultural landscape

The question of identity and its relationship with heritage within a modern state has also been influenced by the issue of commercial development and land rights, which have emerged as significant issues after the inclusion of the state of Sarawak in the nation state of Malaysia. The profound association the Kelabit people had with their homelands was seriously disrupted in the decades since WWII. During the 1960s, the Confrontation with Indonesia threatened Kelabit longhouses close to the border, and many of the inhabitants of these villages were evacuated and sheltered in Bario by British and Commonwealth forces. At the conclusion of the war, when Sarawak joined the Malaysian Federation, the Kelabit people experienced an imposed physical disconnection from their kin residing across the border in Kalimantan. In 1967, Harrisson estimated that there were at least ten times more Kelabit people living on the Kalimantan side of the border than there were in Sarawak.[12] This resulted in a disconnection across national borders, but it also meant that those Kelabit people who had been moved to the Malaysian side of the border needed to be adequately accommodated, and in this process lands that were traditionally owned by the Bario Asal were reassigned to the newcomers. In the years that followed, during which the current leadership of the RKS were attending schools and universities, the continuity of traditional land management order and the broader cultural values associated with the land and the forest were further undermined by various amendments to the legal mechanisms through which the Sarawak government controlled and administered native lands. The relationship between identity, land and the politics of development in the Kelabit Highlands therefore influenced the trajectory of the project, and this needs further contextualisation.

In the early 1970s, the Sarawak Land Code distinguished some native rights, and in 1976 the Sarawak Land Consolidation and Rehabilitation Authority (SALCRA) was established to reallocate the use of native land.[13] This contributed to the heated contestation over access to and control of natural forest resources. The very real consequences of this power became apparent in the 1980s, when the Sarawak government 'forced the Iban of Batang Ai to resettle in a new area' to make way for the State's first hydroelectric dam.[14] During this development project, 33 longhouses were relocated, and while there was some compensation for the people effected, as John Phoa observed in 1996, the resettlement resulted in the 'loss of their ancestral land and customary rights, as well as sacred burial grounds and the forest which had been a major source of their subsistence. . . . Such losses [he asserted] are often accompanied by a breakdown of the social fabric of indigenous peoples'.[15] Furthermore, as Sabihah Osman documented, alarm bells continued to ring through the mid-1990s, with the Government's promotion of the *New Concept of Native Customary Land Development*, which was designed to enable private plantation companies to lease native customary lands (from the government) for the development of enormous palm plantations.[16]

Concurrently there were protests by indigenous people against the logging of forests for cheap timber. In Kanowit, Penan led a blockade at Long Ajeng Baram, and in response the government was not afraid to use the law to retain control:

> Besides arresting and charging the indigenous groups concerned, the state government also charged the individual protesters, including a local

environmentalist, Anderson Mutang Urd, a Kelabit, and the leader of the Sarawak Indigenous People's Alliance (SIPA) from Long Napir in Ulu Limbang. He was charged under the Societies Act for alleged involvement in an illegal society and provoking unrest in February 1992.[17]

Incidents such as this have reverberated in the consciousness of Kelabit intellectuals of the RKS who have sought to relocate themselves and their culture in a landscape transformed by development issues. Consequently, they have been concerned to investigate their spiritual and cultural connections to the land in the Highlands, both natural and agricultural, and in this process they found local and international allies arguing for the profound importance of environmental conservation in Borneo.

In 1996, the fourth biennial conference of the Borneo Research Council was held at the University of Brunei Darussalam, and a key topic amongst the delegates was the need to recognise that environmental conservation in Borneo was a transnational issue. Forests that stretched across national borders were referred to as 'transfrontier linkages', and the topic of the discussion was the idea of creating a biodiversity conservation area comprising the Lanjak Entimau wildlife sanctuary in Sarawak and the Bentuang Karimun national park in West Kalimantan. It was reported that at that time the site in West Kalimantan comprised an area of 16,000 square kilometres, making it the largest block of protected rainforest in Borneo; additionally, it also was emphasised that approximately 10,000 indigenous people, including Kelabit, Kenyah and Penan, lived in and around the area. Peter Eaton, a contributing author of the book *Borneo: Change and Development* (1992), reported that recognition of the cultural and spiritual connections that these people had with the environment was fostering research into forest resources, agricultural practices, oral traditions and histories, and the cultural mapping of village land boundaries using participatory processes and GIS techniques. He optimistically stated that it was 'anticipated that the status of the reserve would change to that of a National Park, a designation more appropriate to human activities in the area and the possible development of tourism'.[18] Furthermore, he wrote:

> The Kayan Mentarang reserve [another site] stretches to the Sarawak border and the establishment of the proposed Pulong Tau park in the Kelabit Highlands in Sarawak would enable another transfrontier conservation area to be established, with the possibility of much of central Borneo eventually becoming an internationally protected area.[19]

In this context, the importance of the international community in lending support to Kelabit heritage-making and to the ecology of the region is tangibly illustrated even if these particular transfrontier linkages were never formalised. It was perhaps easier for each nation state to pursue its own conservation agenda with the assistance of UNESCO. In the year 2000, for example, the Gunung Mulu National Park, which stretches up-country beyond the palm oil plantations that dominate the hinterland around Miri, was inscribed on the UNESCO World Heritage List for the significance of its biodiversity and karst features.[20] This World Heritage site is in close proximity to traditional Kelabit lands, and the town of Bario is approximately 100 kms to the southeast of the park. By 2006, the idea of an integrated approach to the conservation of Borneo had progressed from the discussions of transfrontier linkages to a more ambitious integrated conservation agreement between the three nations of Borneo. After facing down a proposal for the world's largest palm oil plantation, the World Wildlife Fund (WWF) and the Governments of Malaysia, Indonesia and Brunei committed to the *Heart of Borneo* declaration to conserve and sustainably manage the intact forests of central Borneo, which include the traditional lands of the Kelabit and other indigenous tribes. The *Heart of Borneo* project has facilitated the implementation of a number of programs that have exposed a range of transnational cultural heritage issues.[21]

A galvanising issue for the Kelabit people had clearly been the contestation over access to natural resources in the surrounding district. In response, some members of the community have tried to address the legal case for land ownership. This strategy was led by Dr Ramy Bulan, a lawyer and academic based at the University of Malaysia, who was, during the development phase of the Kelabit Highlands Community Museum, a Senior Vice President of the RKS. As Bulan pointed out in 2003, the Kelabit traditionally navigated the Highlands using established paths and local knowledge, but in the 1990s they were obliged to secure border agreements where access to land and resources were negotiated with their neighbours. This process required a formal process of defining territory, and the methodology for doing so foregrounded 'the issue of the place of maps and mapmaking in a culture that not long ago knew only of mental maps'.[22] Bulan argued that the Kelabit have deep cultural and historic connections to the land, but because of the lack of written records, the case needed to draw upon other sources that included 'factors of history, oral traditions, cultural practices, [and] permanent and semi-permanent marks on the physical landscape'; this combination of understanding intangible and tangible heritage, she wrote, 'constitute records [that] must be taken into account in considering the question of the Kelabits' connection to an occupation of the land'.[23] Recently the evidence that underpins this argument has been bolstered by survey and documentation fieldworks. Research carried out by the McDonald Institute for Archaeological Research, University of Cambridge, under the leadership of Graeme Barker, has revisited the documentation of Kelabit cultural sites, including burial sites marked by substantial stone structures and monoliths. These were first described by Edward Banks in 1937, and their significance was reiterated by Harrisson in the 1960s.[24] This research project reasserted the importance of the landscape as a 'cultural and historical artefact' and through reasserting the significance of the Highlands as 'a cultural landscape' has given more weight to the significant relationship between land and identity.[25]

The town of Bario itself has great meaning in contemporary Kelabit culture and is the principle gateway to the protected and threatened forests of the Kelabit Highlands. The town is the centre of a constellation of seven longhouses and has grown into a regional depot serviced by an airport, telecommunications and the Internet, and since 2012, an unsealed road to the coast. Recent developments in or close to the town, such as the mechanisation of farming practices and the growth of roads and traffic, have followed an aggressive economic development agenda. Events in 2014 further exposed the need to formally recognise and document the heritage values of the cultural landscape in and around the town. There appeared to be some urgency to address this because the Sarawak government was proposing a substantial town-planning scheme for Bario. The plan conceived Bario as

Figure 6.1 Stone Monolith, Kelabit Highlands, June 2012

a highland recreational town for the benefit of Malaysians with a scenic hilltop drive surrounded by holiday villas, and a central shopping district featuring twin rows of modern shop houses. The approach appeared to be one of top-down imposition rather than consultation. This exposed the fact that there has been no effort to date to undertake any systematic documentation of local heritage values, particularly those concerning the mountain and land usage within the town precinct, and thus no conservation issues appeared to have been considered to inform this development plan. Also highlighted was the fact that there continued to be a threat to the achievement of native sovereignty through land use legislation. It appeared that the museum project, with its focus on heritage conservation and community engagement, gained some traction within the local community and as a result it gained momentum. This was in contrast to the government's perceived lack of meaningful consultation concerning local natural and cultural heritage values that are bound up with a significant cultural landscape.

Notes

1. Simon Wilmot, *World Within No More*, VEA Australia, New Zealand, Bendigo, Victoria, 2013.
2. Tom Harrisson, 'Tribes, Minorities and the Central Government in Sarawak, Malaysia', in Peter Kunstadter (ed), *Southeast Asian Tribes, Minorities, and Nations, Volume 1*, Princeton University Press, Princeton, 1967, pp. 321–322.
3. Ooi Keat Gin, 'Education in Sarawak During the Period of Colonial Administration 1946–1963', *Journal of the Malaysian Branch of the Royal Asiatic Society*, Vol.63, No.2, 1990, pp. 35–68, p. 40.
4. Ibid, 1990, p. 35.
5. Ibid, 1990, p. 40.
6. Ibid, 1990, p. 43.
7. Details on the Colombo Plan are available on the Australian Government, Department of Foreign Affairs and Trading website, http://dfat.gov.au/people-to-people/new-colombo-plan/pages/new-colombo-plan.aspx, accessed 29 May 2017.
8. Ooi Keat Gin, 'Education in Sarawak During the Period of Colonial Administration 1946–1963', *Journal of the Malaysian Branch of the Royal Asiatic Society*, Vol.63, No.2, 1990, pp. 35–68, p. 51.
9. Ibid, 1990, p. 44.
10. Interview with Lucy Bulan recorded in Bario, Sarawak, June 2012. Simon Wilmot, World Within No More , VEA Australia, New Zealand, Bendigo, Victoria, 2013.
11. Poline Bala, 'An Engagement with "Modernity"? Becoming Christian in the Kelabit Highlands of Central Borneo', *Borneo Research Bulletin*, Vol.40, 2009, pp. 173–185, p. 182.
12. Tom Harrisson, 'Tribes, Minorities and the Central Government in Sarawak, Malaysia', in Peter Kunstadter (ed), *Southeast Asian Tribes, Minorities, and Nations, Volume 1*, Princeton University Press, Princeton, 1967, p. 328.

13 Evelyne Hong, *Natives of Sarawak, Survival in Borneo's Vanishing Forests*, Institut Masyarakat, Malaysia, 1987, pp. 54–58.
14 Sabihah Osman, 'Globalization and Democratization: The Response of the Indigenous People of Sarawak', *Third World Quarterly*, Vol.21. No.6, Capturing Globalization, December 2000, pp. 977–988, p. 980.
15 John Phoa, quoted in, Sabihah Osman, 'Globalization and Democratization: The Response of the Indigenous People of Sarawak', *Third World Quarterly*, Vol.21. No.6, Capturing Globalization, December 2000, pp. 977–988, p. 980.
16 Ibid, 2000, p. 983.
17 Ibid, 2000, p. 986.
18 Peter Eaton, 'The Conservation of Cultural and Environmental Diversity in Borneo', *The Geographical Journal*, Vol.163, No.1, March 1997, p. 118.
19 Ibid, 1997, p. 118.
20 UNESCO World Heritage Centre, *Gunung Mulu National Park, Description*, http://whc.unesco.org/en/list/1013/, accessed 10 November 2013.
21 Sarah L Hitchner, Florence Lapu Apu, Lian Tarawe, Supang Galih@Sinah Nabun Aran and Ellyas Yesaya, 'Community-Based Transboundary Ecotourism in the Heart of Borneo: A Case Study of the Kelabit Highlands of Malaysia and the Kerayan Highlands of Indonesia', *Journal of Ecotourism*, Vol.8, No.2, 2009, pp. 193–213.
22 Ramy Bulan, 'Boundaries, Territorial Domains, and Kelabit Customary Practices: Discovering the Hidden Landscape', *Borneo Research Bulletin*, Vol.34, 2003, pp. 18–61, p. 19.
23 Ibid, 2003, p. 19.
24 See, Edward Banks, 'Some Megalithic Remains from the Kelabit Country in Sarawak with Some Notes on the Kelabits Themselves', *Sarawak Museum Journal*, Vol.4, No.5, 1937, pp. 411–437. And, Tom Harrisson, 'Inside Borneo, The Dickson Asia Lecture', *The Geographical Journal*, Vol.130, No.3, 1964, pp. 329–336, p. 331.
25 Karen L. Coates, 'Forest of Broken Urns: Borneo's Unexplored Past Is Dying by the Chainsaw', *Archaeology*, March/April 2007, p. 34.

7 The development of the Kelabit Highlands Community Museum

Introduction

The aim to encapsulate a culture – a pervasive, evolving, ever-changing set of values, beliefs, attitudes and behaviours – and package it for the purpose of representation, preservation and to foster economic generation, presents many challenges. The process of identifying the key aspects to highlight in cultural representation and defining how to communicate the outgoing image of traditions, customs and local vernacular is an organic process; a continual evolution, much as a culture is in constant change and development. Kelabit intellectuals recognise this as being rooted in their hybrid identity, and accept the influences and complexity this brings to their culture. Nevertheless, the process of heritage-making is one of construction, and the museum concept grew in steps from firstly discussing the ideas, to creating community support, designing and constructing the space, collating the information and finally realising the interpretation through design. It is a process in which the trust between all participants needed to be negotiated until the transformation of cultural heritage (as understood by a community) into a representation (that can be understood by an audience) was achieved.

In some circumstances museums are 'invaluable resources because of their potential to foster local identity in a time of increasing globalisation and to be representational bodies engendering a sense of belonging to the groups who make and use them'.[1] Given the availability of resources, it has been argued that museums have the ability to assist in the development of regional renewal and to empower community members through providing a representation of history and a commentary on how the community has changed and evolved. Community museums may also be flexible, growing and organic entities that are closely connected with the surrounding environments, including the culture, economy and demographics of the people they serve.[2] The KHCMDP makes transparent this complexity and required a process through which community expectations were managed, while the process traversed contested approaches to representation and communication, in an effort to make the museum an ongoing, sustainable initiative. To explain how the work was undertaken, this chapter provides a detailed account of the planning and methodology that was used and discusses some of the associated issues that emerged.

Developing structure and representation through design

Much of the behaviour of visitors who attend museums is reactive as they unconsciously respond to space, colour, shape and form; that being the design of the exhibits.[3] In community museum spaces, where professional expertise may be lacking, there may be varying understandings of working with displays and technology. For example, graphic panels may have too much text, type may be too small, displays may have objects or labels at heights not accessible to everyone or the narrative does not reflect the display.[4] Volunteer staff can be limited in their capacity to implement long-term strategies and may find it difficult to construct suitable displays. This impacts on the experiences that visitors have in galleries and is critical for their engagement and learning. For example, those visitors who encounter old technology in a museum space may associate the exhibit with outdated content and the key aim of the gallery may be undermined.[5]

Although designers are well placed to work with the creation of representation in the timeline of history where identity continues to change, the challenging conversations of identity and representation analysed in museology theories and practices throughout this book are equally contested in design practice. As identified by Myles Russell-Cook, who discussed the concept of decolonising design,[6] the western concept of design predicates that the individual is the creator, yet this project defies this notion, identifying the Kelabit community as the designer. This new paradigm means authorship and ownership of a narrative, potentially thousands of years old, and drawing on the design practices of indigenous people whose designs are imbedded in ritual and cultural meaning, requires a new way of thinking and working. The means of communicating through design, rather than through oral or written modes, requires bringing local expertise to the design practice and situating this in their location in a respectful manner.

However, the experiences of the authors and the KHCMDP highlights this was not always an equal, uncontested collaboration. Instead it was a swinging pendulum of negotiation and learning from each other until the Kelabit community were comfortable with the outcome and representation. Elizabeth Simone Reitsma, a designer, when working with three indigenous communities in Sarawak, Malaysia, identifies designers need to be aware of the impact of their role as a designer.[7] This requires recognising the past experiences of external input on the community and how this may impact the design. Reitsma recommends developing tasks that make the visions of the community a reality, allowing flexibility for adjustments as required and maintaining patience to let the community guide the process. These recommendations were adhered to in the KHCMDP and naturally developed as the DU team, RKS and community groups worked together. Leadership was based in the community, space was granted between programs for the community to be proactive and guide the development, and this ensured, as much as possible, control sat with the community.

The representation of Kelabit cultural heritage and identity involved engagement with the community to define heritage values and designing a tangible representation of these values. In essence, this was a process of transforming the intangible into something tangible. The 2003 UNESCO *Convention for the Safeguarding of the Intangible Cultural Heritage* defines intangible heritage thus:

> the practices, representations, expressions, knowledge, skills – as well as the instruments, objects, artefacts and cultural spaces associated therewith – that communities, groups and, in some cases, individuals recognize as part of their cultural heritage. This intangible cultural heritage, transmitted from generation to generation, is constantly recreated by communities and groups in response to their environment, their interaction with nature and their history, and provides them with a sense of identity and continuity, thus promoting respect for cultural diversity and human creativity.[8]

For the KHCMDP, the design process of turning the intangible into something tangible was the transformation of ideas and opinions into physical designed artefacts. It included incorporating an extensive list of aims and ambitions that were articulated in a discussion document created on behalf of the RKS by Nikki Lugun in 2011.[9] These included: to educate others and pass on traditions; to preserve materials in personal collections; to document culture and indigenous knowledge; to assist tourism and commerce ambitions; and to transfer technology skills. To achieve this, the KHCMDP used applied research which aimed to utilise the intellectual capital that resided within the community, to assist in determining the most appropriate means to communicate intangible heritage values through tangible constructs. In turn this incorporated contemporary design theory, in which it is argued that representation is constructed from a series of signs and symbols.

Culture embodies the best that has been thought or said of a group in society, maintained through shared values and systems of representation.[10]

This is reflected in the discipline of semiotics, in which it is argued that the codification of signs such as words, images and sounds are learnt as we grow up in a culture.[11] Since all cultural objects convey meaning and all cultural practices depend on meaning, they also make use of signs, underlying codes and conventions. Each culture has its own complex set of rules, prohibitions, permissions, values and classifications. Gunther Kress explains that these codes appear as normal and natural to the general population and as a result we accept these sets of rules as the natural order of how things should be.[12] People who share a language, a history and a way of life have connections that are very deeply ingrained. This impacts communication; the aim of which is for the recipient to receive and understand the message intended.

Research partnership: Rurum Kelabit Sarawak and Deakin University

As an established community organisation of some years, at the commencement of the KHCMDP the RKS was already experienced in the organisation of projects which employed academic engagement and partnerships to achieve shared goals. Nevertheless, it was believed that the community had also been subjected to unbeneficial extractive methods of research. As Roger W Harris wrote:

> Research tourism in Bario began as a purely extractive process; researchers chose their topic and the location in which to study it and they engaged local residents to assist them. Their presence contributed to the local economy through accommodation, lodging and the hiring of staff as research assistants. At the end of their stay, they departed and published their findings, mostly with little subsequent reference back to the community. The knowledge that was generated may or may not have been useful to the community. In some instances, the published findings did not necessarily accord with the opinions of the community.[13]

Harris had worked very closely with the RKS on the application of new technologies in the Kelabit Highlands and was a partner in the establishment of eBario. At the start of the KHCMDP it was clear that the community shared his preference for partnerships which aligned with the community's own goals, and in which they had a high degree of agency. Harris' suspicion of research tourism was in turn shared by Nikki Lugun, who echoed this concern when she wrote an introductory briefing paper that was forwarded to Sweet in 2011.[14] This paper outlined a vision for a community museum which would belong to and support the social development of the Kelabit people. Lugun writes:

> Over the years, countless researchers and academicians from all over the world have made their way into the remote Kelabit Highlands in the center of Borneo to conduct valuable anthropological, ethnological, botanical, cultural and socio-economic studies. In addition, hundreds of photographs have been taken of the people of the Kelabit Highlands. All these lie in prestigious universities and museums as well as private collections all over the world. Sadly, very little, or none of this [sic] studies have been made available to the people living there. The Community Museum Project is a pioneer project which will be situated in Bario, the largest settlement within the Kelabit Highlands and will serve as an important element in the access, preservation and continuation of the tribal group's culture and history.[15]

The discussion document created by Nikki Lugun adeptly outlined a vision that was centred on reclaiming cultural heritage assets for the benefit of the Kelabit community. It also identified some gaps in the professional expertise of the community that would need to be addressed if the aim of creating a museum was to be achieved. Lugun identified that:

> The community members realised that they did not have the resources to achieve the goals of the Community Museum Project alone. They will have to approach various organizations to assist them, recognizing that many of these organizations could bring significant intellectual, archival and technological resources to such a project.[16]

In addition, it was stated by Dato Isaac Lugun, very early in the project, that:

> It must be done professionally and for it to be something sustainable and for us to involve the authorities or even the community, I think it is important for the concept, for the proposal, to have credibility. You only have credibility if you have the experts in the field help you develop the proposal. Without credibility, I think it is difficult to get buy-ins from the various stakeholders, or even from the government, or even from the museum authorities in Malaysia, or when we want to enlist fundings (sic). So, it has to be a credible concept that they recognize, that they can see.[17]

Thus, the RKS initially sought a dialogue with DU concerning the broad possibilities of creating a Kelabit museum, with this document providing the starting point for the initial discussions. Nevertheless, with the community's suspicion of research tourism in mind, there was a question of how the partnership would be constituted so as to ensure that the community benefited from the project, especially when it became clear that the creation of a community museum required the RKS to lead an extensive process of consultation and to negotiate a community-wide strategic plan to realise their ambition. This also posed a question for DU: if the University participated in helping to shape the project, the project also needed to account for the involvement of its staff and other resources.

As the dialogue between the RKS and the DU team developed through meetings and community consultation, the scope of the project became more ambitious, and it was reiterated that the community needed assistance in understanding the operational requirements of contemporary museums, and the relationship that was fostered between the RKS and DU became more critical to the project. It is worth saying that although the parties arrived at the start of the project from very different perspectives in 2011, the participants shared some common knowledge of the trends in cultural politics in Southeast Asian heritage discourses, and as the project developed a coherent focus emerged where participants across a range of disciplines were united by their ideological commitment to the idea that local communities ought to have agency in a wide range of conservation processes. Thus, there was an imperative that the KHCMDP incorporate effective community participation and capacity building that would be essential for the sustainability of the museum.

As the project developed, the authors (their associates and students) worked with the RKS in an advisory capacity but also in very practical ways. The working relationship that evolved between the RKS and DU may represent a form of what Amar Galla has termed 'cross-cultural heritage management' in which a mutual respect developed between the participants who were focused on the goal of creating this museum.[18] At the beginning of the project this was effective in part because the DU personnel had no other official affiliations in Sarawak (although Sweet had conducted research at the Sarawak Museum and had broader project experience in cultural heritage management, tourism and museums in Southeast Asia). It should be noted too that the parameters of responsibilities were fairly carefully respected, and as specialist consultants the DU team provided advice to the RKS exclusively. This was seen as beneficial because, as has been noted by others, the success of rural development projects in Sarawak had in the past been compromised by competing allegiances.[19]

In order to formally address the issue of research tourism and community agency, the partnership between the RKS and DU was formally confirmed through a Memorandum of Understanding created 19 February 2013.

Nevertheless, this relationship remained understated and was not widely publicised. There was a sense that the interest and actions of western activists concerning issues of forest resources and indigenous land rights had given rise to a perception within the Malaysian government that some forms of engagement with indigenous people in Borneo constituted foreign interference in development issues.[20] For this reason, it was essential for the project that the RKS was solely responsible for negotiating the political, social and economic challenges concerning the foundation of the museum. This was entirely appropriate and sensible because a central thread of the project was the shared aim to maximise the opportunities for community representatives to be agents in the processes of cultural representation, and for conceptualising the project in such a way that would assist the long-term sustainability of the museum.

The KHCMDP was seen as a community driven initiative with benefits tied directly to the Kelabit community, supported by local ownership of the process and the results. Nikki Lugun had identified five aims for the KHCMDP: first, to educate others and pass on traditions; second, to preserve materials already in private collections; third, to document culture and indigenous knowledge; fourth, to assist tourism and commerce ambitions; and fifth, to transfer technology skills during documentation.[21] These aims were primarily conceptualised with reference to the concept of a 'virtual museum' that had been discussed among some members of the RKS. Essentially this approach to conservation was envisaged as a means of extending the social development role of the eBario website, which had principally promoted tourist services in the Kelabit Highlands. Once representatives of the RKS and DU met, the concept of a physical museum presence was tabled and the idea began to be developed, and this meant that the parameters of the KHCMDP were substantially expanded and the project became more complex and interdisciplinary. The guiding principles outlined by Lugun aligned closely with the areas of expertise at Deakin University. As the methodology for advancing the project was discussed, the DU academics considered how best their skills and knowledge might be used to assist with fulfilling the clearly defined aims of the community. It was felt that an adherence to supporting the expectations of the community would lead to a strong relationship between the RKS leadership group and the DU academics.

While different communities may share a range of motivations for developing a museum concept to assist with the coordination of their cultural resources, the practice for realising each community's vision is often variable and context-specific. This means that each museum development project will be shaped by unique challenges, including in this case the challenge of maintaining a collaborative cross-cultural engagement. From the outset, the KHCMDP involved participants from a broad spectrum of experience who were primarily located in Malaysia and Australia. The DU team included representation from a diverse but cognisant range of disciplines, including cultural heritage and museum studies, film, architecture and design studies. During the course of the project between 2011 and 2016, members of the DU team visited Sarawak on multiple occasions. During these visits face-to-face meetings and extensive community consultations were held, and three intensive fieldwork programs were conducted. The use of fieldwork was an applied research methodology that was used to advance through the steps of the project. Each of these programs was conceived as a response to the needs of the community and was supervised by DU staff and utilised students in a range of research and creative activities.[22] The first program (15–28 June 2012) undertook a community-wide scoping exercise of cultural assets to identify examples of tangible and intangible heritage, focused on community-wide consultation, identified potential aims of capacity building and produced a draft strategic plan for the development of the project. The second program (15–30 January 2014) focused on understanding issues concerning the built environment and conservation in Bario and delivered conceptual architectural ideas for the museum building itself; and during the third program (3–13 December 2015), the participants researched the potential of interpretation and communication content that had been articulated through prior community participation and piloted ideas for the development of internal communication strategies and branding for the museum.

Study abroad program used to facilitate fieldwork research

In part, the approach to this project was informed by the discourse concerning 'public pedagogy', a term developed by Henry Giroux.[23] He defines academics that disseminate expert knowledge to the general public for public good as *public intellectuals*.[24] Giroux argues it is the obligation of intellectuals to be open to communities, connecting their theories to practice to make them valuable to the general public. These theories link with concepts of social change, distributing knowledge for the purpose of public adoption of ideas. Public intellectuals therefore work with a broad range of people, and as Jennifer Sandlin, Michael P O'Malley and Jake Burdick have written, their jurisdiction is 'centered around but not confined to the classroom [and they are concerned with] forming alliances beyond the classroom with students, parents, and community organisers to link critical imagination with public activism'.[25] This association with a range of participants may lead to a transformative engagement that addresses a particular social problem, and involves a process of critical change or, as in the instance of the KHCMDP, provide a means of empowering a community to make its own decisions.

This project applied the notion of public pedagogy to cross-cultural circumstances, and furthermore, in doing so, it reiterated the desirability of applying intersecting concepts of theory and practice. This recognised that the project provided an opportunity to interrogate theoretical questions into the process of developing working practical applications.[26] The approach was inspired by Kimberley Curtis, who has drawn attention to the need for universities to revise pedagogy and embrace hands-on learning around public agency.[27] He has argued that this would create a culture where participants believe change is possible and communities understand their ability to craft change. Underpinning this is the contention that mutual learning creates a sense of hopefulness in collective action and shared responsibility. Typically intellectuals can assist with orchestrating the circumstances in which the community has agency in the organisation of events, an approach that challenges the usual one-directional flow of teaching and learning, so that the learning dynamics are more interactive.

Study abroad programs sit at the intersection of pedagogy and public intellectualism. In some contexts, study abroad programs may be called education abroad, learning abroad, international learning mobility, outbound mobility or student exchange. However, in this book the term study abroad program will be used. A study abroad program is a form of experiential learning where students spend a portion of their academic year in a different country while remaining enrolled and receiving credit towards a degree at their home institution.[28] The short-term study abroad programs that are favoured by DU usually run for between 10 and 21 days, and they offer students the opportunity to augment their studies with an experience of cultural immersion, commonly providing structured experiences which are not accessible to an independent traveller. The study abroad programs that were integrated into the KHCMDP took the form of fieldwork research projects and were unique in that they offered an opportunity for the participants to engage with local people in a remote region of Sarawak. The focus of the project meant that the students were able to participate in the processes of understanding heritage-making and museum development in these unique cultural circumstances. In this form of experiential learning, the participants tested ideas, asked questions and explored options, and they gained a valuable understanding of contemporary Kelabit cultural heritage and the associated issues faced by the community (which also informed their work and the development of the museum).

The project therefore utilised a methodology of participatory action research that was designed for change and development. In general, participatory action research is a methodology that is context-specific and fluid, aims to solve real-life problems and acknowledges the diversity of experiences and capabilities of participants.[29] This suited the KHCMDP as it was a way of integrating social investigation, learnings and actions that were focused on assisting the Kelabit community in their social and economic development. It was an iterative research process, whereby enquiry lead to action, then reflection on the actions and then suggested a new line of enquiry.[30]

Action research methodology posits that research activities are dynamic and adaptable, and that a strategy of collaboration may be used to navigate any tension between academic understanding and community goals. Depending on who is involved in each stage, and to what extent, action research becomes participatory action research. 'At its most participatory, researchers engage with participants as collaborators who can inform project design, propose methods, facilitate some of the project activities, and importantly review and evaluate the process as a whole'.[31] It is known for its intent to integrate research into practice, inclusive of the diversity of participants, to ensure agreement with both the process and findings.

Social and political tensions

Much of the process of participatory action research involves collaboration, and therefore it is recognised that tensions can exist in the relationships between the researcher and the researched, especially where they have different aims and ambitions for the project; and for this reason, the relationship of the participants plays an important role in all phases of the project.[32] Action research commonly takes three stages; inquiry, action and reflection.[33] Each of these may overlap and intersect. As action research is a social and political act, it is important to conduct respectful, open, honest and timely communication to maintain and strengthen participant relationships.

The relationship between the RKS and the DU team was both supportive and challenging and was tested by a range of issues. From the outset it was expected that the Kelabit community ought to initiate the research goals and retain control over their participation in the project, and that the protocols that governed the research would be aligned with the values of their culture.[34] However, there was friction within the community and fears were expressed by Kelabit individuals during consultations that these aims were not being respected. This issue was resolved to some extent through mutual support. RKS leaders and the Deakin academics revisited the issue of researcher intervention to try to ensure that community agency was maintained. In addition (and consistently), the RKS leadership sought to clarify that in their opinion the project benefited from the guidance provided by the academics from Deakin University. It was explained that far from being excluded from the process, the community was being encouraged to participate; and that it should gather ideas, discuss the best path forward and help to navigate a solution that would best suit the desired outcomes.

There was, however, a challenging structural issue in the relationship between the participants, which was associated with the intermittent flow of financial and professional resources. This meant that the dynamics of the management of the project ebbed and flowed between the RKS and DU. Although the goal was for equal partnership between the researchers and the community, inevitably the academics from DU were implicated in the internal politics of the community, and RKS was connected to the dynamics of the Australian higher education sector through the requirements of DU. For example, although attempts were made to work to define outcomes prior to each fieldwork program, the expectations of the RKS and the DU team were sometimes misaligned. Difficulties were enhanced by the distances between parties and the cross-cultural nature of the project that resulted in an unclear determination of the tools and resources that were available. Additionally, geographic distances and competing responsibilities between members of the Kelabit community also delayed the decision-making process and revealed different expectations amongst RKS members. This was evident in the fieldwork that was focused on architecture, where some Kelabit leaders were expecting DU expertise to provide definitive plans for the building, whereas the DU team planned the available time to research and offer a range of ideas and conceptual design solutions to be used to promote discussion amongst the wider community.

In part the tensions arose because of the competing interests between the project and the formal requirements of the study abroad scheme. Academic leaders are obligated to consider student wellbeing and university requirements of academic content and accountability. This may work as a discreet program, but it posed a challenge when it was incorporated as a methodological tool in the community development project, as it became apparent that the participants had trouble attending to the community's expectations. This was further complicated by the diversity and competing voices within the Kelabit community, and the lack of confidence within the DU team to negotiate local politics, allegiances and interests in the longhouses of Bario. This made it difficult for the visitors to clarify or understand the range of community expectations and apprehensions within a limited time. In this event, the issue was addressed to an extent at a large community consultation meeting held in Miri, where the architectural and design ideas were presented for consideration by the participants who attended. Measured in terms of participation, the meeting was a great success, but when the DU group departed Malaysia, there was some reflection about the focus of the architectural program. Nevertheless, it became apparent in the following months that the discussions and feedback from the Miri meeting were a turning point in gaining the engagement of the Miri-based Kelabit community across a range of significant design and interpretation issues. Furthermore, the creative architectural work undertaken in Bario was profitably fed into the internal RKS discussion about the aims and design of the physical building, and certainly influenced the final outcome of the museum.

Despite the existence of a planning document which provided a map of the development process, the progress was retarded to an extent because the participation of members of each of the parties was based on voluntarism. That is, the RKS and community members who directly engaged with the project often balanced other commitments, as did the DU team. There were thus significant breaks between periods of fieldwork activity, when funding was gathered in Australia and when discrete projects were organised. It was sometimes unclear who was driving the next stage of the project. The timelines for organising the fieldwork, for example, were subject to the need to secure grant funding from external agencies and were further complicated by formal enrolment and compliance requirements, including the selection and preparation of the student participants. Thus, although initiated predominately by RKS, the commitments made by individual Kelabit participants to manage some activities within a fieldwork program were tested by the sequence of events. Similarly, the participation of DU academics was subject to their ability to balance other commitments.

Yet, it is clearly understood this project provided benefits to not only the community but all participants, including academics and students. Academics were provided privileged insight into a real-life challenge for a community, while at the same time affording the opportunity to examine more closely the intersection of theory with practice. Students were offered a unique learning environment as they were confronted with complex stakeholder concerns. The project connected young with old, academic with community and traditional with contemporary. The community were challenged to define a representational image of themselves while the visiting academics and students respectfully demonstrated ideas through the architecture, exhibition and branding possibilities, all of which had occurred as a secondary consideration to the day-to-day lives of the participants. In this event, much had been learnt about the challenging nature of representation and identity creation for an indigenous, marginalised community, and what can be achieved with inherent determination.

Notes

1 Andrea Witcomb and Verena Mauldon, 'Local Museums and Cultural Policy: Reforming Local Museums?' *Culture and Policy*, Vol.7, No.1, 1996, pp. 75–84, p. 81.

2 Yuha Jung, 'Building Strong Bridges Between the Museum and Its Community: An Ethnographic Understanding of the Culture and Systems of One Community's Art Museum', *International Journal of Inclusive Museum*, Vol.6, No.3, 2014, pp. 1–11.
 3 John H. Falk and Lynn D. Dierking, *Learning from Museums*, AltaMira Press, Walnut Creek, CA, 2000, p. 113.
 4 Nina Simon, *The Participatory Museum*, Museum 2.0, Santa Cruz, CA, 2010, p. 296.
 5 Bruce Wyman, Scott Smith, Daniel Meyers and Michael Godfrey, 'Digital Storytelling in Museums: Observations and Best Practices', *Curator*, Vol.54, No.4, 2001, pp. 461–468, p. 464.
 6 Myles Russell-Cook, 'Decolonising Design', in *NGV Triennial 2017*, Council of Trustees of the National Gallery of Victoria, 2017, pp. 204–211, p. 204.
 7 Elizabeth Simone Reitsma, *Dynamics of Respectful Design in Co-Creative and Co-Reflective Encounters with Indigenous Communities*, Doctoral Thesis, Northumbria University, Newcastle, 2017.
 8 UNESCO, *Convention for the Safeguarding of the Intangible Cultural Heritage*, 2003, https://treaties.un.org/doc/Publication/UNTS/Volume%202368/v2368.pdf, accessed 3 November 2017.
 9 Nikki Lugun, *Narrative and Rationale, the Kelabit Highlands Community Museum Project*, Unpublished concept paper, 2011.
10 Stuart Hall, *Convention for the Safeguarding of the Intangible Cultural Heritage*, Sage Publications, London, 1997, pp. 2–4.
11 Arthur Berger, *Making Sense of Media: Key Texts in Media and Cultural Studies*, Blackwell Publishing, Malden, MA, 2005.
12 Gunther Kress, *Communication and Culture*, University Press, New South Wales, Australia, 1988, p. 12.
13 Roger W. Harris, 'Tourism in Bario, Sarawak, Malaysia: A Case Study of Pro-Poor Community Based Tourism Integrated into Community Development', *Asia Pacific Journal of Tourism Research*, Vol.14, No.2, 2009, pp. 125–135, p. 131.
14 Nikki Lugun, *Narrative and Rationale, the Kelabit Highlands Community Museum Project*, Unpublished report, 2011.
15 Ibid, 2011.
16 Ibid, 2011.
17 Simon Wilmot, *World Within No More*, VEA Australia, New Zealand, Bendigo, Victoria, 2013.
18 Cited in Christina Kreps, 'The Theoretical Future of Indigenous Museums', in Nick Stanley (ed), *The Future of Indigenous Museums: Perspectives from the Southwest Pacific*, Berghahn Books, New York and Oxford, 2007, pp. 223–234, p. 229.
19 Dimbab Ngidang, 'The Politics of Development in Longhouse Communities in Sarawak, East Malaysia', *Development in Practice*, Vol.5, No.4, 1995, pp. 305–312.
20 Peter Brosius, 'Prior Transcripts, Divergent Paths: Resistance and Acquiescence to Logging in Sarawak, East Malaysia', *Comparative Studies in Society and History*, Vol.39. No.3, 1997, pp. 468–510, p. 471.
21 Nikki Lugun, *Narrative and Rationale, the Kelabit Highlands Community Museum Project*, Unpublished report, 2011.

22 The fieldwork which were run through the Study Abroad Program assisted in addressing the Deakin University costs.
23 Jennifer A. Sandlin, Brian D Schultz and Jake Burdick, *Handbook of Public Pedagogy: Education and Learning Beyond Schooling*, Routledge, New York, 2010, p. 2.
24 Jennifer Sandlin, Michael P. O'Malley and Jake Burdick, *Mapping the Complexity of Public Pedagogy Scholarship: 1894–2010*, Sage Publications, 2011, p. 355.
25 Ibid, 2011, p. 356.
26 See, Meghan Kelly, 'Public Learning Derived from Institutional Learning: The Case Study of the Kelabit Highlands Community Museum Development', *Journal of Public Pedagogies*, Vol.1, No.1, 2016, pp. 6–17.
27 Kimberley F. Curtis, 'Creating a Culture of Possibility: A Case for Engaged Pedagogy', *Humanity & Society*, Vol.36, No.4, 2012, pp. 354–373, p. 359.
28 See, Davina Potts, 'Understanding the Early Career Benefits of Learning Abroad Programs', *Journal of Studies in International Education*, Vol.19, No.5, 2015, pp. 441–459, p. 442.
29 John Mackenzie, Poh-Ling Tan, Suzanne Hoverman and Claudia Baldwin, 'The Value and Limitations of Participatory Action Research Methodology', *Journal of Hydrology*, Vol.474, 2012, pp. 11–21, p. 13.
30 Davydd J. Greenwood and Morten Levin, 'The Relationships Between Universities and Society Through Action Research', in Norman K. Denzin, Yvonna S. Lincoln (eds), *The Landscape of Qualitative Research: Theories and Issues*, Sage Publications, Thousand Oaks, CA, 2003, p. 149.
31 John Mackenzie, Poh-Ling Tan, Suzanne Hoverman and Claudia Baldwin, 'The Value and Limitations of Participatory Action Research Methodology', *Journal of Hydrology,* Vol.474, 2012, pp. 11–21, p. 13.
32 Hal A. Lawson, Christine T. Bozlak, James C. Caringi, Janine M. Jurkowski and Loretta Pyles, *Participatory Action Research*, Oxford University Press, Oxford and New York 2015, p. 126.
33 See, Stephen Kemmis, Robin McTaggart and Rhonda Nixon (eds), *The Action Research Planner*, Deakin University, Geelong, Victoria, 1988. And, Stephen Kemmis and Robin McTaggart, 'Participatory Action Research: Communicative Action and the Public Sphere', in Norman K. Denzin and Yvonna S. Lincoln (eds), *Handbook of Qualitative Research*, Third Edition, Sage Publications, Thousand Oaks, CA, 2005, pp. 559–604.
34 Meredith Gibbs, 'Toward a Strategy for Undertaking Cross-Cultural Collaborative Research', *Society & Natural Resources*, Vol.14, No.8, 2001, pp. 673–687, p. 678.

8 Detailed encounters

Introduction

During this project the authors worked with the RKS in an advisory capacity, and they also contributed to its progression in very practical ways. For this reason, their personal interactions with many members of the community have informed this interpretation of events. The information presented below has been constructed from various sources of documentation that were generated during the life of the project and is deliberately presented here as a narrative that relates significant aspects of the process. This account draws upon a range of material including formal and informal conversations, recorded interviews, notes and images and published material, as well as a curated exhibition that showcased photographs, text and the mini-documentaries of Kelabit events that were made by students in Bario. The exhibition provided an insight into the experiences and recollections of the student participants.[1] These sources represent the wealth of material that the authors and their associates created from the inception of the project in 2011. The information that was generated attests to work undertaken, which included key actions such as the initial scoping exercise to test the feasibility of developing a museum in the Kelabit Highlands, the use of community consultation to identify, support and develop strategies for the implementation of the museum and participatory conceptual design-oriented consultations to develop ideas for the architecture and surrounding precinct, heritage interpretation and identity branding. Published articles and media that were generated by the DU team to document the progress of the project have also been used as aide-mémoire to support this account.

The KHCMDP was an interdisciplinary project that drew upon the experiences of a DU academic group, and thus this account incorporates a variety of perspectives. Each member came to the project with distinct knowledge and experience: Sweet's research was focused on museology in Southeast Asia and he had worked with UNESCO and ICCROM on community-based projects in the region. He had also designed fieldwork in the region for DU cultural heritage students. In 2011, he received an ICOM Award for International Relations in the field of museology for *The Lampang Temples Project* he led jointly in Thailand with UNESCO and Chiang Mai University. Architect Susan Ang had experience conducting cross-cultural study abroad programs with Malaysian colleagues and had conducted research into socially responsible and community informed design practices in Southeast Asia. Meghan Kelly's doctoral thesis was focused on cross-cultural visual communication design, and she had worked internationally on identity creation and representation. Filmmaker and academic, Simon Wilmot, had produced documentaries about the issues faced by indigenous communities in Australia and the region. In this project, therefore, these individuals acted as informed facilitators and advisors and they brought a range of theoretical and policy-based concepts to the project. Collectively their involvement guided the decision-making process.

Project overview: 2011–2016

The project presented in this book occurred from 2011 to 2016. Essentially, the project took on three stages: identifying ideas, confirming those ideas and finally unpacking those ideas into a communicable structure. During this process there were multiple visits to the region over a five-year period. The KHCMDP was initiated by the Kelabit Community, and the outline expressed a clear interest in conserving their cultural heritage. With the assistance of Jan Drew, an educational consultant based in Malaysia, the RKS was introduced to Sweet, and he was invited to visit the region in 2011 to discuss the concept and viability of creating a community museum in the Kelabit Highlands. It was agreed that there was a need to understand the geographical and cultural contexts in which the project was to be pursued.

In early 2012 Sweet travelled to Bario. The aim of this visit was to discuss the idea of developing the community museum with the Council of Village Headmen. According to local protocol, this initial meeting was critical. The Chair of the meeting was RKS executive member, John Tarawe (who was at the time the local representative to the Baram District Council). At the meeting the concept was discussed and it was suggested by Tarawe that the implementation might benefit from utilising the expertise of the DU team. It was proposed that the DU team would work in partnership with representatives from all the longhouses, and therefore it was critical that there was widespread community support for the concept and a broad willingness to participate. It was pointed out that this was an ambitious aim because despite an apparent awareness about the immediate risks to the preservation of Kelabit culture, local participation could be impeded by economic circumstances; many residents in the district were busy subsistence farmers and hunters. These realities meant that it was critical that all the Headmen present at the initial meeting confirmed their willingness to support the project and to actively encourage others to participate if they were able to do so. In the event, the response to the proposal was very positive, with Tarawe describing the management plan as a 'smart partnership'. The enthusiasm expressed by the Headmen was a particularly important result because it reinforced the vision of the RKS, which was to investigate the concept of developing a community museum and how it might bring benefit to the community.

It was therefore agreed that the first stage of the project should focus on undertaking a foundational community-wide scoping exercise that aimed to understand the extent to which the residents of Bario and outlying villages understood and supported the idea of creating a community museum. It was agreed that this would also to some extent be a capacity building exercise designed to assist a range of people to begin to articulate the significance of their cultural assets – the objects, events, knowledge and stories that embodied tangible and intangible cultural heritage values. This was seen as essential for strengthening the skills within the community that would help it to attain greater agency in the process of representation. This first step in the consultation process also provided the DU team an understanding of the kinds of local human and other resources available in Bario, which the project might be able to utilise. As a result of the meetings in Bario, it was determined that the RKS and DU would undertake a joint fieldwork project in 2012.

Building support by involving the community

The first fieldwork research project took place in June 2012, and the DU team participants included staff and post-graduate students from cultural heritage and museum studies and undergraduate film and television students. Each student was required to fund most of their own program costs while the cost of the two staff members, Sweet and Wilmot, were supported by the School of Humanities and Social Sciences, the School of Communication and Creative Arts and Deakin International. It was anticipated that the participants would benefit pedagogically through experiential learning, undertaking a range of challenging tasks that contributed to the advancement of the program. The aim was to conduct consultation to investigate the capacity of the community to contribute to the museum and start to identify key heritage values of Kelabit culture that might be presented in the museum, both tangible and intangible. Cultural heritage students were charged with the role of explaining the concept of a community museum

98 Detailed encounters

and facilitating and engaging in a discussion with local people about the significance of their heritage. Through this the students were able to promote the project extensively amongst all longhouse communities and were apparently able to gain widespread support for the museum concept. Film and television students were required to create a series of mini-documentaries. This provided an opportunity for community members to tell significant stories in their own words and to demonstrate culturally specific activities, thus potentially providing a valuable resource for the conservation and interpretation of Kelabit heritage. Through this process local people attained a high degree of agency in explaining the significance of long held cultural practices. In addition, a half-hour documentary film titled *A world within no more*[2] was produced by Wilmot about the aims and genesis of the project; this documented the valuable contributions to this consultation process of a range of local people.

A crucial outcome of the 2012 fieldwork program was that there was a clear confirmation of community support for the museum concept in Bario. It also demonstrated that there was material in the community that could be used to showcase Kelabit society. A key notion that was expressed in discussion about the project with community representatives was the feeling expressed by Kelabit participants that as their culture continued to adapt and change, a community museum concept could be a useful means to positively engage succeeding generations in the preservation of their cultural heritage. In addition, the museum would act as a vehicle for sharing this culture with domestic Malaysian tourists as well as international visitors. Through this consultation process it also became apparent that the rurally dispersed members of the Kelabit community shared similar aspirations to those expressed by their RKS leadership. All had started to envisage a community-owned facility that would create and nurture a range of cultural programs in which they could meaningfully participate.

This support was essential to underpin both the viability and sustainability of the project, and the first phase of the research conducted in Bario gave the RKS considerable confidence to go on to facilitate further community consultation meetings in Miri and Kuching, and these attracted between 15 and 50 participants.

Articulating the physical representation

A key outcome of the scoping exercise was a report that outlined a staged development process and offered recommendations. The diagram below, taken from the report, demonstrates the generalised concepts that were informed by the fieldwork that had been completed. Each of the phases were developed in consultation with the community and, once in tangible

PHASE 1: Project definition

- To understand the commitment to a community museum through discussion and consultation with the RKS and the Council of Headmen
- To develop a scoping process with an emphasis on community consultation and a participatory model of sustainability
- Plan the fieldwork and scoping campaign

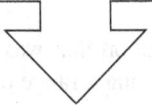

PHASE 2: Fieldwork in Bario and surrounds
Deakin University in collaboration with the Kelabit community

- Community consultation focused on the roles of the museum
- Feasibility assessment of cultural assets and human resources
- Piloting the preparation of audio-visual material
- Draft discussion document prepared by the Deakin University team

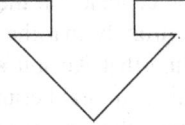

PHASE 3: Museum definition and policy development
Kelabit Community, collaboration

- Define a Statement of Purpose for the community museum
- Define community and identify visitors and target audience
- Identify and leverage funding opportunities
- Draft policies and processes, including management structure, community engagement processes, collections policy and collections management process

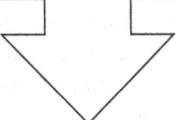

PHASE 4: Implementation
Kelabit community, collaboration

- Develop a brief for the design and fit-out of the museum building in accordance with the current museological discourse and sustainable cultural tourism
- Build collection in accordance with collections policy and exhibition and interpretation goals
- Develop exhibitions and museum program, including special events and heritage trails
- Finalise policies and processes
- Finalise staffing and management structure

Figure 8.1 Kelabit Highlands Community Museum Development Plan 2012

form, this determined the agreed program and provided a framework for ongoing relations and terms of reference to guide the project. While the collaborative nature of the plan remained a constant principle, the envisaged phases deviated and evolved as the project became more interdisciplinary. Thus the project developed through the employment of additional expertise to guide approaches to the built environment, exhibition design and branding.

The report included information that was intended to inform the community about ways of approaching a range of issues concerning the effectiveness of museum buildings in tropical conditions and the utilisation of digital interpretation both online and in museum galleries. It also identified some challenges and limitations that might retard the planning and implementation of the museum, including the financial capacity to maintain the enterprise, the cost and availability of construction materials, the energy requirements of a generator or solar power, the impact of climate and environmental conditions on displayed artefacts and the physical, educational and virtual accessibility of the content. On the basis of the research fieldwork, the report also argued strongly that the museum concept needed to advance from an understanding that Kelabit society is a living and continually evolving entity in which cultural heritage was being actively redefined. As a consequence of this, the report posed a series of suggestions for documenting, recording and safeguarding intangible heritage. Thus, the mini-documentaries were conceived as potentially very valuable assets to be utilised by the community. However, it is worth acknowledging that in the event the limitations of power, climate and technology were not well understood, and this exposed some doubts about the feasibility of using this material effectively in museum interpretation.

Nevertheless, the next step of the project pursued a strong focus on designing a building. This meant that there was a need to consider the architectural functions of the museum, understood in terms of representation and conservation, as well as the incorporation of appropriate facilities to be effective as a site for community engagement, learning and visitor service. To pursue this phase of the project, a DU team including Sweet, Ang and Kelly returned to Sarawak to participate in another series of community meetings that were organised by the President of the RKS, Dato Isaac Lugun. It was significant that these meetings were not limited to Bario, but were also convened in Miri and Kuching, because this effectively widened the pool of participants from rural people, who are predominately farmers, to include those Kelabit people residing in urban centres; and, in the event, the more diverse skill set that was evident in these sectors of the community proved to be very useful to the project. These meetings incorporated reports on previous activities, and facilitated discussions of concepts and ideas that might be pursued in the future. Each meeting included a screening of Wilmot's documentary film, *World Within No More*,[3] which adeptly presented the RKS rationale for pursuing the museum development project. The film also incorporated the views of many members of the Kelabit community and highlighted their concerns for the preservation of their cultural heritage. To any doubters in the audiences, the film had the effect of demonstrating the serious intent of the museum development project, and it seemed to boost the willingness of people to participate in the consultation process that followed each screening.

Emerging from this consultation process was a strongly expressed interest that the next stage of the project should incorporate the creation of conceptual designs for an appropriate museum building. It was agreed that the spatial requirements would be dictated by the functions the facility would serve, incorporating a number of possible open public spaces and closed support spaces. Essential to the aims of the community, the building would require a gallery space for display of artefacts and photographs; storage area and conservation room for the protection and maintenance of items; resource library for the collation and dissemination of written materials; multipurpose space for meetings, craft workshops, storytelling, music and dance performances; a visitor information centre as a return site for general information and tourism opportunities; and a shop for sale of items (i.e., maps, books, handicrafts, souvenirs), which could potentially be used to raise revenue for the museum and/or other local projects. In addition to these factors, it was also important to consider the building as a hub of community activity for the sharing and celebration of culture, bearing on the museum's role and enduring relevance.

This led to the development of the second fieldwork program, which was conducted in January 2014, and was focused specifically on architecture, and it aimed to conceptualise the physical building. In this case the program was supported by an Australian Government funding initiative to develop student competencies and knowledge of countries in Asia.[4] So in addition to the DU students from the Master of Architecture program, the group included architecture students from the International Islamic University Malaysia, under the tutorship of Associate Professor Nurul. The focus of the program was to provide guidance to the community through creating conceptual designs of the museum building.

Prior to undertaking fieldwork, members of the DU team conducted extensive design focused research. The architecture team, for example, completed a Design Master Class which investigated options and ideas to understand the limitations and opportunities of creating a structure in the tropical conditions of Borneo. The process included investigating the macro and micro climatic conditions, local traditions of craftsmanship, building materials and vernacular architecture, and artist practice and iconography. Professional architects acted as mentors as the participants conducted a preliminary site analysis, and created site models and context plans.

Before departure the academic and student group discussed in depth possible ways in which to engage the community and encourage conversation. Referring to the participatory action research methods of engagement, it was agreed the facilitators, Ang and Kelly, would suggest as a starting point the community consider how they wanted the museum to engage the community in an ongoing way. However, during the architecture fieldwork community consultations, this carefully considered approach proved ineffective, as the community chose their own engagement process – to great effect. Initial comments brought forward ideas of four-dimensional exhibits, aspects of touch and feel, an online presence, performances, spaces to showcase artistic talents, media support and seeking the engagement of high profile Kelabit people or celebrities who had visited the region. As the consultation evolved, the conversations became fragmented and participants divided to create their own subgroups. The DU team best served as note takers, clarifying information and teasing out ideas[5] as valuable information surfaced in subgroup conversations.

Three key ideas were tabled; two followed a structure of key topics and a third considered the chronological order of historical events. To explain these further, to develop content and the subsequent impact on the built environment, a group of community members suggested to break down the information into key topic headings; our journey, our history, contact with the outside world, Christianity, transition, transformation and where they are now. These topics were broken into subcategories of information. 'Our journey' would require pictorial, visual and physical demonstrations; 'our history' would consider the legends and cultural representations of music, stories, songs, dance and games; and 'contact with the outside world' would seek the stories and methods of when the outside world first contacted the remote community.

Many stories emerged about firsthand experiences of meeting people outside of the Bario region. One such story was told where a Headsman recalled the first sight of someone outside the community parachuting into Bario during WWII. Most people ran away in fear, but as a young man he was intrigued and instead of running, held his ground in fascination. The parachutist landed and eventually presented the young boy with chocolate, eating some himself before handing the rest to the young boy. This was the first time the Kelabit, now an elder, had met someone who was not Kelabit, and eaten chocolate. The importance of this story and how it could be used in the museum development could not be defined during the community consultations; however the significance of the experience was not lost

Detailed encounters 103

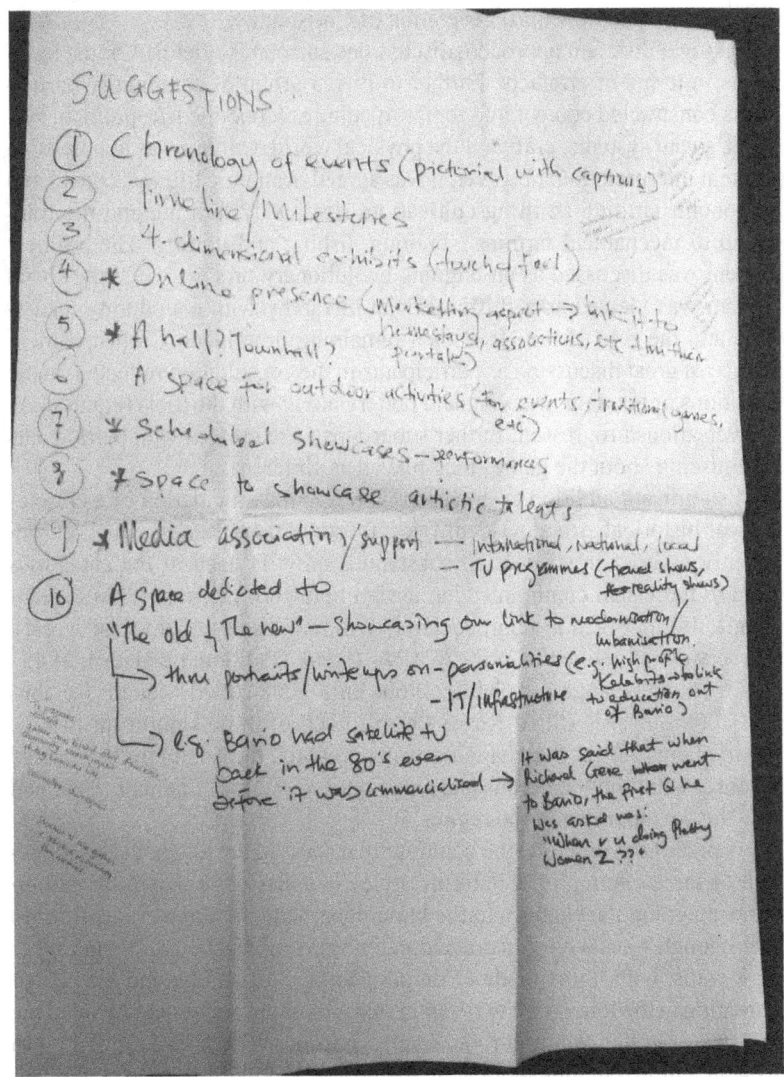

Figure 8.2 Community consultation notes, Miri, January 2014

with the community and discussions surrounded who still had parachutes in their personal collection of memorabilia, prompting further thoughts to be discussed and documented. In addition, the subcategory of 'Christianity and the evolution of the Kelabit belief system' was expanded as a topic to consider the transformation from the old belief system of headhunting to the first, second and now third generation of Christianity.

Taking a different approach, discussions surrounded defined 'must have' items in terms of artefacts. Further to this, a group of community participants constructed content into topics of culture, economic life, political systems, social systems, craft and the physical world. Culture was a topic open to great interpretation; however, it was agreed economic life was considered to contain farming (shifting cultivation, rice paddy farming and the transition to mechanical farming), hunting, fishing and trading. The political system was discussed as an ongoing evolutionary process while the social system was viewed as a shifting social hierarchy with community leadership and the role of the Headsmen remaining prominent. Craft became a source of great discussion as participants in the consultation reflected on the traditions of beading, weaving and pottery along with the tools required. As conversations progressed, further subgroups were created with participants reminiscing about the games they played as children.

A significant addition to the discussion was the articulation of a chronological historical structure identifying four key time frames, which consequently assisted in structuring substantial shifts in each of the categories used in the visual communication design fieldwork program (culture, economic life, political system, social system, craft and the physical world). These were explained as prior to 1944 (titled Traditional Kelabit), 1945–1960s (titled Changing Kelabit), 1960s until 2008 (titled Modern Kelabit) and 2008 onwards (titled Roads Open). Each of these significant historical moments reflect the changing ways in which the community accessed resources, building materials and techniques, farming equipment, ideas and saw the development of the region.

As part of the timeline, the community discussed the longhouse as reflective of the evolution of Kelabit lifestyle. Sketches were drawn by participants mapping the changes to the building structure and materials. Prior to 1944, longhouses were constructed in timber with thatched roof and timber bark walls, with floors made of timber planks. Storytelling and the role of parenting in the longhouse was communal, commonly conducted around the fire (tawa) in the common room (dapon padung). The tawa was central to Kelabit culture, significant in maintaining social order in a large communal space. Large logs were collected for the fire – the larger the log, the stronger the man – and log lengths in the dapon padung determined space allocation for families. Boys and young men ran through the corridors and logs were placed outside of houses to show how many girls were dating from each longhouse. The community noted from 1945 until the mid 1960s, chainsaws led to smaller logs sawn. Although timber was still used to create longhouse structures, timber planks could now replace bark for the longhouse walls and shingles replaced thatching for the longhouse roof. There was more use of bamboo as it was easier to cut when the axe was introduced. Storytelling diminished with the introduction of formal western-style education and tattoos and earrings were not as fashionable.

However, the most significant time, according to the community, was 2008 onwards, when roads were built linking Miri with Bario and new materials became available. Buildings became larger and families were choosing to develop private quarters extending from the common room (dapon padung). Beds, seats, lounge suites, amongst other domestic items, could be driven to Bario and transformed the living quarters of the community. There was an increase in the economic opportunities for the region and tourism became a key economic driver. The rapid transition that occurred post the Confrontation in the 1960s and through to today, reflected the Kelabits' strong attachment to the concept of progress.

Returning to the central focus of the architecture fieldwork program, the aim was to determine ways in which the community might use this space in order to continue and encourage Kelabit cultural practices. The topics and categorisations to emerge with community participation assisted in framing the building requirements. This challenging, and significantly important aspect to the project, identified as necessary a gallery space, storage area, conservation room, resource library, multipurpose room, information centre and exhibition space. As a result, the students were able to design ideas based on these requirements; however, these concepts were not practical and instead succeeded in demonstrating to the community that with everything taken into account, the building, conceptually, would become very large.

In addition, it was discussed that if the museum were to have a role in conserving Kelabit culture, it would need to successfully engage with the next generation of Kelabits, to the extent that they would continue to return and be actively involved in the programming and development of contemporary content. This issue was raised with the four younger members of the community group, aged between 18 and 29, who were introduced to the project in the 2013 community consultations. The contribution from the younger generation highlighted a desire by them to use the space in their own way; to create an annual event for their own demographic, or to use for social occasions. This initiative was met with support from the community, and added further to the design considerations.

Emerging from the younger Kelabit community members were obvious tensions between the values of representation as identified by the leadership group of the Kelabit community and the younger generation's understanding of what it means to be Kelabit. The children of the leadership group were unfamiliar with the background of the stories told and were

Figure 8.3 Architecture student concepts, January 2014

interested in aspects that were commonly not discussed in their presence. These include the headhunting era prior to WWII, a period of Kelabit history rarely acknowledged, and the destruction of some longhouses during the 1960s Confrontation. These topics were noted as important but were still not discussed openly during the community meetings.

The discussions, in themselves, were an important outcome. A great deal of work was completed in Bario, and between projects the DU team returned to Australia with plans to develop ideas further as RKS continued their internal dialogue. This was an orchestrated process over the five-year engagement. Although the ideas of the students were strengthened by the honest and open discussions of the community, continued RKS discourse was required to develop the final outcome. When the museum building was completed in 2016, the finished structure can be seen as a reflection of the collaboration and a carefully calculated first step in what will become the Kelabit community museum development precinct.

Interpreting history and heritage

Further projects were drawn from the architecture fieldwork program community consultations in January 2014 and embedded in the Visual Communication Design program at Deakin University. In 2014 and 2015, third-year design students, as part of their curriculum, explored the visual representation of Kelabit identity as they considered the branding for the museum and the design of the exhibition space.

One of the outcomes of the first meeting with the Village Headmen in Bario was a conversation about words in the Kelabit language that most closely aligned with the idea of a museum. After some debate, it was agreed that the word *teripun*, which means a safe storage place for food or possessions, most closely approximated the preservation activities of a museum, such as the Sarawak Museum, which they knew well. The use of a *teripun* in longhouse villages is longstanding, and this reinforces the theory that the Kelabit have maintained a culture of the selective care and preservation for their material culture over many generations. Anthropologist Christina Kreps has documented the traditional preservation activities and practices of similar Dyak longhouse activities in Kalimantan, and has argued that these processes resemble a form of 'curatorial practice' which embodies a finely grained heritage consciousness.[6] During the second fieldwork program, the design group was able to pick up the idea of the *teripun* and develop it further, and over time the name stuck within the community. As conversations continued, a name for the museum emerged: **Teripun Tauh: Kelabit Highlands Community Museum**. *Teripun* being the Kelabit word for *place of safe deposit* and *Tauh* is defined as *storage place*. Combined they were reflective of *our archive* or *our safe storage space*. While the methodologies of community participation in heritage projects may need to be scrutinised, it would be fair to say that in this case through the process of discussing the meaning of the *teripun*, the Headmen were able to articulate the similarities (and differences) between their own long held cultural practices and the role of the museum. The community appeared to be very comfortable with the name **Teripun Tauh**, and over the course of further consultations, it replaced the term 'the museum'.

Visual communication design students, based on information from previous fieldwork, were able to draw on the cultural connections of the community, including *Batu Lawi*, longhouses and traditional beading and weaving to develop conceptual branding strategies. Over 150 design ideas emerged during this two-year period, and through a student driven evaluation process, fifteen designs were returned to the community for consultation. The community responded with positive reviews for all of the designs; however, as an example of the limited communication between DU and RKS between study abroad programs, the feedback from the community endorsed the visual communication design ideas but did not provide constructive criticism or further guidance to progress the project, highlighting the need to conduct a third fieldwork project in December 2015.

In preparation, Sweet returned to Bario, June 2015, to discuss a third fieldwork program, and to view the progress of the construction of the museum building; it was a significant and emotional moment to see the timber building under construction. The building was located in the town centre and was an adapted version of some of the conceptual designs presented to the community in the architecture fieldwork program. The building was smaller in scale but was designed and sited to provide the capacity to be expanded in stages. The work was overseen by RKS executive member Nelson Kebing, a government architect based in Kuching, who had also been involved in some building restoration work at the Sarawak Cultural Village. Kebing travelled to Bario from Kuching regularly to oversee the project, and he was assisted by Lian Tarawe, a local Bario businessman and a talented draftsman who had drawn up all the building designs and plans. The design had adapted the idea of creating a building with a silhouette of two roofs which echoed the twin peaks of the mountain, *Batu Lawi*. It also expressed the look and feel of the vernacular architecture of the region. The ground floor incorporated a symbolic central fireplace, which is the traditional heart of the longhouse. And the design also sought to address functional requirements, including providing for an information desk, meeting rooms and an open space and stage for the demonstration of cultural practices. The construction of the timber frame was very hands-on, with Kebing and Taware working closely with a local building contractor. Over the course of a few days in Bario, Sweet, Kebing and Taware discussed a range of practical issues concerning the interior design of the museum, in particular focussing on issues such as physical access and the technical requirements of a second floor gallery.

In anticipation that the building would be completed in time, the direction for the third fieldwork program was agreed upon with other representatives of the RKS and preparations commenced. The Australia Malaysia Institute (AMI), Deakin University Global Mobility program and the students themselves collectively provided funding support for the third fieldwork program. This was led by Sweet and Kelly, with participants from Cultural Heritage and Museum Studies and the Bachelor of Creative Arts (Visual Communication Design) tasked with addressing and developing concepts for heritage interpretation and branding the museum, and implementing communication and exhibition designs.

There was a concern that the building would not be available for students to use as an exhibition space. Nevertheless, it was agreed that the focus of the program was to present to the community a structural way of representing their historical content with the facilities available. Drawing on the research and outcomes of previous fieldwork programs, including a wide-ranging collection of data and resources such as photographs, recorded interviews, meeting notes, drawings and personal conversations,

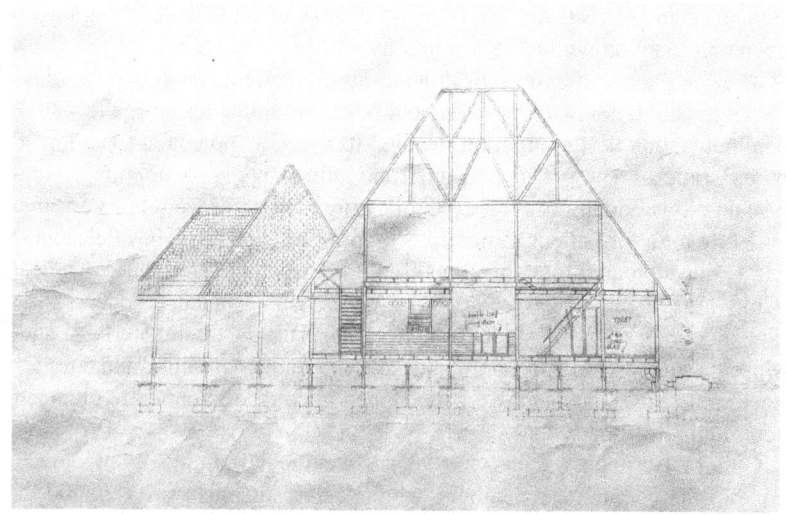

Figure 8.4 Construction drawings by Lian Tarawe, 2015

Figure 8.5 Kelabit Highlands Community Museum under construction, December 2015

students were to create a comprehensive display of content, encouraging an open conversation within the community.

The complexity of options in structuring information was collated during the architecture fieldwork program and further examined prior to the visual communication design program, leading to five key topic areas developed by the students. These were presented and refined by the community during consultations, and it was agreed the following topic areas would serve as the structure for information: Komuniti (Community), Pelajaran mey Pelancongan (Education and Tourism), Pudut ulun (Craft and Performance), Tanaq (Cultivating the Land and the Forest), Upacara istimewa lem ulun lun Kelabit (Timeline). A pair of students – one student from Cultural Heritage and Museum Studies and one from the design program – was allocated a topic. Each topic and the content were developed in collaboration with volunteer community members.

Cultural Heritage students were keen to capture the complexity of knowledge of the community members, while design students were required to refine the content to suit the limited paper and exhibition space requirements. In each instance, this process was a new experience for the students and required a delicate negotiation of the depth of content versus the space to fit the content. In addition, it was a requirement to have the text in English and Kelabit. Although translation into Malay was also a priority, writing content in a third language was not possible due to the availability of a translator and the limited space in the exhibition. The student cohort found it challenging to present all of the potential stories to demonstrate Kelabit identity and instead, in hindsight, were only able to touch the surface of possibilities for the narratives that could be told. It was hoped this first exhibition could serve as a starting point to present for debate the central themes.

A key issue was resources and the expectations the DU team had balanced with what was available. A significant challenge of this fieldwork was the capacity of the solar power unit and the lack of strength to charge all of the computers and power the printer. Achieving the design outcomes required multiple appliances running consecutively. A petrol generator was necessary, leading to an increased demand on petrol and several petrol purchases. Bikes were hired by students to conduct research and community visits, yet punctures were common, and the local bugs were attracted to the artwork as much as visitors. The exhibition was during rainy season, so weather, transportation and accessibility impacted on outcomes. Even with these factors, the students were able to produce a substantial, albeit temporary, exhibition for the community, held in the open community space. It was hosted in the reception area of the museum and was well received by those who attended.

Detailed encounters 111

Figure 8.6 Interpretive material, Visual Communication Design Fieldwork, December 2015

The exhibition was seen as a success where the student cohort was able to present an interpretation of Kelabit identity based on the consultation and community collaboration. It echoed the position of Zahava Doering, who explained that the 'exhibitions that visitors find most satisfying are those

112 *Detailed encounters*

Figure 8.7 Exhibition in the Kelabit Highlands Community Museum, Bario

that resonate with their entrance narrative and confirm and enrich their existing view of the world'.[7] In this case, the design process translated the narratives drawn from community participants into a tangible visual expression that was intended to promote an ongoing dialogue on ways in which to achieve authentic Kelabit representation. Interviews were conducted during the day with visitors. Some comments were appreciative, such as, 'I'm happy to see uncle and grandfather in the exhibition'. Other comments were educational, declaring the exhibition 'covered most things – very informative'. It was understood the interpretive material produced would be used to question and re-evaluate a meaningful exemplification of Kelabit identity; however, the exhibition provided clarification to many, and was seen as an authoritative view of what was important to represent. Concerns over a lack of agency in representation, a major motivation for undertaking this project, were alleviated when, for the first time, the village had a Kelabit generated view of their history presented back to them which could be evaluated. This view was an agreed understanding, helping to differentiate between fact and fiction, and as stated by one visitor, served as a very powerful form of community consultation itself. The exhibition was deemed important to help the community talk about what they collectively understood as their history. A further comment concluded that things were changing rapidly and to capture the content in a display was a great starting point as it opened the community's eyes to the unfamiliar.

Notes

1 *The Kelabit Highlands Community Museum Development Project Exhibition* took place in April 2013. The opening night included a screening of Simon Wilmot's documentary film, *World Within No More*. The event was attended by a representative of the Consulate of Malaysia.
2 Simon Wilmot, *World Within No More*, VEA Australia, New Zealand, Bendigo, Victoria, 2013.
3 Ibid, 2013.
4 The New Colombo Program was an initiative of the Australian Government to increase the knowledge of the Indo Pacific in Australia by supporting undergraduate students to study, take internships or complete research in the region. Details are available on the Australian Government, Department of Foreign Affairs and Trading website, http://dfat.gov.au/people-to-people/new-colombo-plan/pages/new-colombo-plan.aspx, accessed 29 May 2017.
5 Carina Katigbak, Meghan Foley, Lauren Robert and M. Katherine Hutchinson, 'Experiences and Lessons Learned in Using Community-Based Participatory Research to Recruit Asian American Immigrant Research Participants', *Journal of Nursing Scholarship*, Vol.210, No.2, 2016, pp. 210–218, p. 214.
6 Christina Kreps, *Liberating Culture: Cross-Cultural Perspectives on Museums, Curation and Heritage Preservation*, Routledge, London, 2003.
7 Zahava D. Doering, 'Strangers, Guests, or Clients? Visitor Experiences in Museums', *Curator*, Vol.42, No.2, 1999, pp. 74–87, p.82.

9 Concluding remarks

Introduction

This account of the development process of the Kelabit Highlands Community Museum and Cultural Centre has focused on the relationships between indigenous identity, heritage conservation and cultural representation in contemporary Southeast Asia. This study adds depth to our understanding of the ways in which minority communities in the region are engaging with their cultural heritage, including investigating the role of indigenous knowledge systems, and weighing up the potential benefits of aligning with international frameworks and approaches to the conservation of tangible and intangible heritage. In particular, this book provides a detailed case study of the heritage-making efforts of the Kelabit community of Sarawak and Malaysia, situated within an understanding of the historical, political, economic, ethnic and religious contexts.

At the core of this endeavour is the heartfelt ambition of the Kelabit people to seek agency and ownership of the conservation and representation of their cultural heritage. The central aims of this community-led project therefore distinguished it from state cultural production. In comparison to the well-established Sarawak Museum, for example, there were clear differences in the level of resources available to the community and in the mechanisms through which the project evolved. The KHCMDP, therefore, is a unique historical record because it documents the contemporary cultural dynamics of the process of heritage-making undertaken by a complex community. It was recognised at the commencement of the project that the process of museum development offered an opportunity to negotiate and define community values according to an internal measure of authenticity, and to prioritise aspects of ethnic identity; a goal that members of the community have been grappling with for many years. This comprehensive account of the museum development in the Kelabit Highlands has therefore documented and explained an innovative grassroots conservation process undertaken by a marginalised indigenous community. In particular, the book has highlighted issues arising from the project that are of broader significance to understanding the potential of indigenous agency and the consequent representation of values and identity through museum design.

The task of achieving cultural democracy

At the start of this project, the RKS leadership were focused on the need to act quickly to address the loss of knowledge caused by 'the passing over' of older members of the community who harboured precious memories of society before WWII. The project was therefore designed with some urgency to advance Kelabit agency in the management of their cultural heritage assets. From the beginning, community consultation was employed as a key part of the project methodology, as the mechanisms to enable this were embedded in village governance structures and long held social practices. This methodology reflected the responsibility of the RKS to be sensitive to the variety of community needs and ambitions.

Although it was perhaps understated, there was a view and a determination that if Kelabit culture was to survive and thrive, this project must assert a belief in 'cultural democracy'. Given the political context, it was critical that the museum was distinguished by community action and its progress was the result of shared aspirations. For this reason, the project was envisaged by RKS as one that was independent from the state and relied upon very little government patronage, although this did not rule out collaboration. The vision of the RKS was shaped by an historical familiarity with museums, high levels of western education and an understanding of current forms of indigenous representation, including the roles of cultural villages within the tourism system in Southeast Asia. Thus, the RKS executive committee was strategically focused on exploring museology as a tool to meet their own conservation needs and representational ambitions.

This strategy is in part explained by the values held by the Kelabit people, who recognise a cosmological situation in which their view of themselves and their contemporary culture has been influenced by an apparently incongruous range of historical, social and spiritual experiences. They cite and articulate very clearly the influence of their own traditional knowledge system, Christianity, western education and the political and economic policies of Malaysia and Sarawak as the most important influences. These experiences had perpetuated a degree of cultural hybridity in understandings of Kelabit identity that at various times during the development process was the source of some tension. On the other hand, it also meant that the facilitation of a community-wide dialogue assisted in incubating the advancement of a community-wide approach to heritage-making, which is symbolised by the creation of this museum in the Kelabit Highlands.

The consultation process revealed contestation within the community concerning the articulation and prioritisation of heritage values and expressions of Kelabit identity. Achieving cultural democracy in this case was reliant upon an active program of assisting participants to harness local knowledge and to document traditional practices. In part the participants were motivated to undertake these safeguarding efforts to augment cultural tourism programs that offer some financial rewards, through creating opportunities for visitors and media organisations. The perceived benefits of tourism were something that united many members of the community and became a key consideration to the survival of the project. Nevertheless, as the project unfolded, an understanding of the benefits and risks of relying on tourism as a driver of cultural representation started to emerge. In particular, the participants became more aware of the fragility of their cultural agency and how it might be compromised through commercialisation, and this incorporated a foregrounding of the issue of the maintenance of authority and authenticity in representation and evaluating what was achievable given the location and the limited accessibility to resources. In the community consultation process, although standards and frameworks were discussed, it was recognised that the project was dynamic and that the concepts would continue to evolve in stages as the community negotiated ways to increase their capacity for heritage conservation.

The project applied a process of cultural democracy that was aimed at facilitating the emergence of respected local heritage values. The consultations provided the framework for a dynamic discourse, and with many encounters the participants became more confident in expressing their opinions. The process supported consensus and opened up the possibilities for an innovative museum program based on community needs. For example, competing priorities emerged between the generations, with the younger generation (the children of the RKS executive, for example) offering an alternative vision to the prioritisation of the Christian framing of traditional values that is one of the bedrocks of Kelabit identity. In addition to their parents' and grandparents' focus on the conservation of traditional stories and artefacts, the younger community members expressed the desire to run their own events and to create innovative visual and performance content. This evident contrast (looking back and looking forward) and the ways in which the community began to understand the role and benefits of the museum and cultural centre challenged community consensus and the extent to which the museum could be inclusive and representative of the aspirations of all community members. However, the experience of this project suggests that what this community really desired was the construction of a new social and cultural participatory framework in which people could express their views and in turn reinvigorate the conservation process with the museum being but one outcome of this process. This suggested that, provided the future strategic plans of the RKS are inclusive, encompassing heritage values and contemporary creativity, the museum and cultural centre could develop programs that will be relevant, innovative and sustainable.

The difficulty of capacity building

The KHCMDP incorporated community capacity building across a range of issues that were recognised as critical to museum development and cultural representation. The scope of these efforts was determined by a skills analysis and through research into a range of historical, social and geographical issues. The location of the museum in a remote region with a largely agrarian indigenous community raised questions about the availability of resources that would assist the sustainability of the museum. This was evident through a gap analysis of a raft of operational matters, including inhibiting issues that needed to be recognised in the program planning, such as the difficulty of transporting loan material to the Kelabit Highlands for public exhibition. It was at times hard to envisage the potential of this museum in circumstances where there was inadequate infrastructure and limited access and where the social and economic viability of the village had been undermined by a lack of human resources. This meant that during this project, while the capacity building activities were focused upon and enabled representatives of the community to start to gain confidence in the managerial process of heritage-making, the museum could be planned in accord with their current circumstances and adapt to future needs.

A key capacity building program involved the documentation of local experiences and the role of indigenous knowledge systems and traditions into the process of conservation and representation. The scoping phase of the project, for instance, piloted and applied a research methodology that engaged people in storytelling, so as to document traditional knowledge and reassert a sense of pride in personal experiences. This was critical because it was determined that the management and activities of the museum would depend not only on RKS leadership but also local human resources. The engagement of longhouse residents in storytelling brought people into the museum development process and many became enthusiastic participants. These encounters revealed that when seen from a western professional perspective, some aspects of the criteria used in the heritage significance assessment were problematic. For example, it was at times difficult for some participants to articulate the values of particular artefacts, to start to categorise these items and to prioritise the stories associated with them.

Concluding remarks

To an extent, this may have been due to language, but this reticence, we believe, was also symptomatic of changes in Kelabit society over a number of generations which had eroded the experience of the oral transmission of knowledge, sharing stories and experiences within the community.

Thus, some tensions within the community emerged during recollections of details as different people held different views of the same stories. There was great deliberation between what was fact and what was fiction with differing interpretations of the same events. The overwhelming importance to document these understandings was clearly evident in each of the community consultations; however, it was difficult to document the different interpretations of a single story. The discussions to emerge through the community consultation process proved a valuable format for members of the community to deliberate and expand on ideas, and knowledge, that inevitably strengthened the project. Yet, at times this process was quite confronting for some participants, especially when long-held understandings or orthodoxies were challenged by other participants. There was therefore a need to address heritage interpretation, and to consider an evaluative framework that might in the future underpin the museum's activities.

An aspect of the debate that was centred on the use of the Kelabit language illustrates the complexity of resolving issues of interpretation in these circumstances. There are those who wished to create a written form of the Kelabit language closely reflecting the spoken, and there are others who wished to maintain the complexities of the traditional structures, as documented by colonial anthropologists. Additionally, the retelling of traditional stories based on memory revealed that there were multiple layers of meaning being revealed by different participants. In some other instances, it was difficult to determine the extent to which the aesthetic and spiritual meanings invested in some items were being diluted by their commercial value as a commodity. This raised an important question concerning the relative significance of historical, social and religious events and artefacts, but more importantly it also highlighted the issue of the extent to which the museum managers were prepared and equipped to negotiate local politics and mediate the interpretation process.

While these issues may have posed a problem for some western concepts and frameworks of authenticity, in this project it was accepted that the context and circumstances in which these assessments were being undertaken were rather different, especially in that such exercises were designed to capture information and also to help the participants to understand and potentially exploit the heritage interpretation process. Because the project was not wedded to wholeheartedly following western industry frameworks, it was recognised that while the museum could be established using a traditional museum model as a starting point, it would continue to evolve over time. For these reasons capacity building within this project was focused on building confidence in community-based decision-making processes concerning museum development and cultural representation, and through this it was hypothesised the community would continue to enhance their resources and to progress their conservation efforts in ways that they felt were desirable and manageable.

The challenge of sharing resources through partnerships

This development project was initiated and pursued through a relationship between the RKS and DU. In the initial stages of the project the concept of a community museum was introduced and discussed widely. A scoping exercise, which was focused on an analysis of community resources and the collection of data, was undertaken across many Kelabit longhouses by interdisciplinary teams including representatives of the RKS and DU. The primary result of this initial research was to underpin a strategic plan that provided the community with a staged process through which to proceed, and also with a foundation document which could be used to negotiate with governments and business representatives. In the following stages of the project, when the need for more concrete planning decisions started to emerge, the relationship between the professional advisors and community representatives became more complex, especially as the project gathered momentum and there was more community interest and understanding of its aims and implications. This complexity was accentuated by the local governance system in which decisions concerning this project were negotiated between the Council of Village Headmen, the RKS leadership and other engaged stakeholders, including those community members who resided in Kuala Lumpur, Kuching and Miri. During the project there remained a healthy level of apprehension between the partners, and although this complexity tested the model of project management and the equilibrium between the various roles, events and attitudes, subsequently a fluid partnership developed.

To illustrate the relationship between RKS and DU, we highlight some issues concerning the processes of cultural representation through design. A key challenge of the project was to facilitate a method through which the community was able to share ideas about how the museum would become a dynamic site for the representation of Kelabit culture. For the most part the DU team acted as facilitators to the discussions, offering a range of options. These began with the conceptualisation and design of a museum building. To advance this visualisation, the project incorporated ways of discussing contemporary processes of design and communication, which were focused on critical aspects of museum operations such as a consideration of visitor experience. To facilitate more direct design outcomes, the DU team orchestrated two design-oriented fieldwork programs in Bario and Miri, and these were supported by a range of activities that were conducted in Australia. The methodology was very clear in that a participatory process was utilised in which the DU team initiated and created design concepts during consultation with community stakeholders, and this was followed by a review stage that included prototyping and revision. The exercises conducted during the consultations were used to guide discussions in which the participants shared memories and personal experiences and contributed various points of view. In this way the congregation worked towards a final agreement which was presented in a visual format. In some instances, examples of international museum practice used to inform the community were challenged and or adapted to suit local needs.

In this project design concepts evolved through developments whereby the Kelabit representatives consciously expressed their agency. The participants gained exposure to design focused research and participated in ways that developed their skills through activities such as data collection and the documentation of their own conversations.[1] The members of the DU team who participated in these discussions were then tasked with the role of transforming ideas into creative, conceptual outputs, and then with presenting practical actions to the community for consideration. This iterative design process was critical as it transformed intangible conversations into tangible visual contributions and prompted the next stage of community discussion and debate.

Over the course of a number of years, the project gathered momentum and began to interest more people creating greater complexity in the way in which the project was managed. This was exacerbated by the DU academic team's struggle with competing obligations to the University, hindering their ability to attend regular face to face meetings with representatives of the RKS. The communication between the RKS and DU team was not always effective, and this stalled the timely evaluation of design ideas and concepts. As a result, in some instances, the DU members were not aware of design decisions that were being taken by the RKS or of pertinent information that would assist them in their consultancy role.

Nevertheless, the success of the community consultation process to which both parties were committed was a measure of the cooperation achieved during the project. This was most evident during the fieldwork campaigns, which had very clear logistical and compliance objectives and involved a range of community participants. This interaction resulted in rethinking planned directions and reinforced the consistent ambition for both groups of the project, which was to create a process to initiate the representation of

Kelabit culture. It became clear as the project progressed that the RKS had gained enough confidence to proceed very quickly with achieving a symbolic outcome and were determined to see a building constructed. A member of the DU team visited Bario during the construction phase to review progress, and it was clear that design and construction decisions had been made expediently and organically, confidently drawing upon local knowledge and resources.

The debate surrounding development in Bario

The Kelabit community is famed for its rice production, and many are subsistence farmers and active forest hunters. A more prosperous sector of society includes professional people located in the urban cities of Sarawak who maintain regular connections with their longhouses and the culture of the Highlands. This applies to many of the influential members of the RKS executive committee, who were children growing up in and around Bario in the 1950s and 1960s. These children were sent away to pursue educational and professional opportunities in Miri or Kuching. During this project, it became clear that the community held a diverse range of views concerning economic and social development in the village of Bario. To some extent, this reflected the tension between the maintenance of traditional cultural hierarchies and the changes to the village that were becoming increasingly recognisable through the introduction of contemporary town planning and associated amenities.

Some of the members of the Bario Asal community, for example, were very conscious of the historical circumstances through which their custodianship of land had been eroded. As a result of the Confrontation, Kelabit people from vulnerable villages near the border with Indonesia were evacuated by Commonwealth forces and relocated to the safety of Bario. These people received government allocations of land in the valley that had previously been administered by the Bario Asal, and this upset the conventions of land ownership. As explained by S. Robert Aiken and Colin H. Leigh, all indigenous communities in Malaysia have customary rights in land, and an elaborate body of customs and conventions governs those rights:

> Generally speaking, land is held under various community-based systems of and village community occupies a distinct territory with recognised boundaries, and the household is the basic holder of the rights in land. Tenure arrangements provide for ownership and use of the land but no one has the power to alienate it, and exclusive individual or family property rights usually extend only to the collected or harvested products of the land and to certain fruit trees or other highly prized resources.[2]

These concerns impacted on this project in a significant way, as there was a strong concern within the community about the form and location of the museum building. This began with a debate about whether the museum should be a new building or whether it should be housed in an existing longhouse. It was suggested that it could be located in the Bario Asal, which was already somewhat of a tourist attraction, as the residents regularly hosted cultural events and maintained a handicraft retail outlet. From a conservation perspective, this debate reflected discussions in other locations where the refurbishment of heritage buildings raises issues of museum functionality. It was nevertheless argued that conservation may preserve and exploit the existing tangible and intangible heritage of the Bario Asal. However, the idea of locating the museum within a single longhouse was controversial and divisive, because it conflicted with the RKS aspiration to achieve a united and cohesive representation of Kelabit identity. In practical terms, the community saw the museum building as a connective device between heritage conservation and tourism that would benefit the whole community. The overwhelming preference was therefore to create an icon building in which the form and construction techniques reflected vernacular Kelabit processes. In response to this the DU team undertook research into the conservation requirements of such a facility and worked closely with community representatives to produce architectural concepts for a museum situated in the centre of the village. These designs recognised the tangible and intangible cultural heritage significances of longhouses.

This issue became more complex because it became clear that the proposed site for the museum was contested land. The discussion therefore exposed longhouse allegiances and underscored the tensions that exist around the sensitive and emotive issue of native land rights and land ownership. It revealed that there was a risk that in small communities, such as Bario, the orthodox conventions of communal longhouse structures and extended family associations could become potential fault lines in cultural development and the realisation of projects of this type. Nevertheless, the RKS sought broad community consensus in the museum development process, and subsequently, the organisation was able to negotiate for the use of a site close to the town centre which was owned by the local Government. The location met their aim of enabling a strong connection between the museum, the existing town infrastructure and to the *Balai Raya* or town hall, a place which is often used for community celebrations.

The negotiation of this issue was assisted by the universal spiritual relationship the community has with the Kelabit Highlands. The development process, and a key consideration in the design process, focused on the role of the building as the symbolic entrance to a vast natural and cultural landscape. Thus, the concept initiated by the DU design team was based on the spiritual relationship between natural and cultural values, which incorporated the required spatial relationships for the internal facilities that were required by the community. These designs were presented both on paper and using computer modelling. However, in the first instance, this creative design process produced a very ambitious concept that included all the functionality, amenities and additional spaces required for a modern museum. It included a visitor information centre and research library, a meeting area for public programs, exhibition galleries, performance spaces and essential facilities. Given the circumstances, the concept was unrealistic and it drew a raft of reactions in the community consultations which followed.

Nevertheless, the central theme of the concept was carried forward into the next stage of the design process. This paid strong homage and respect to the majestic and spiritually significant twin peak mountain landmark *Batu Lawi* and its surrounding natural environment. The concept also drew upon the essence of vernacular longhouses, and it was demonstratively representative of Kelabit history, identity and culture. Additionally, its creation delivered an optimistic vision for the future. In response the RKS set about giving tangible form to their aspirations for the museum and cultural centre. The resultant building, adapted by a local architect and draftsman and distinguished by the utilisation of local materials and construction skills, was completed in 2016 and is a scaled down interpretation of the ideas presented during the design process. It was strategically built on a site near the centre of the village where it can physically expand as the community sees fit. Nevertheless, it is noteworthy that the sustainability of a facility of this kind is somewhat undermined by its location on Government land, and this in turn signals that indigenous agency in the processes of heritage conservation and cultural representation remain vulnerable until native title and private land ownership issues are resolved.

Conclusion

Referring back to the argument made by Richard Sandell that museums have the potential to contribute to regeneration and renewal initiatives and assist a community to address its own needs,[3] it is clear that the results of this project support this thesis.

This is exemplified by the shift that occurred with the RKS during the KHCMDP from a narrow object centred approach to heritage conservation to a more purposefully articulated process of community participation in defining and interpreting the relationships between tangible and intangible cultural heritage. The outcome was a significant amendment from the primary concern to collect, preserve and present the physical material from the past, to a more participatory concern of creating a new space and framework for community activities and events, such as art exhibitions and performances, intergenerational storytelling and educational programs.[4]

The initial requirements of determining museum governance and curatorial responsibilities were transformed into discussions of how to encourage engagement and use by the community. For this reason, the focus became securing donations and funding grants, and developing ongoing input from the Kelabit to participate in the creation of content and activities. Over time, with support from external participants, the aim is to build a permanent collection with secured cases and free-standing panels; however, at this stage, the appreciation of culture is developing through community engagement in a space that supports the celebration of traditional songs, dances, language and folklore.[5]

In this respect this project has broader conservation significance because it emphasises the need for greater sensitivity to the hybrid experiences of indigenous cultures, and for the recognition that contemporary heritage-making processes are complex and fluid. In this case, the community's approach to conservation and representation through the museum development project expressed this cultural hybridity, and was shaped by indigenous, Christian and progressively modern experiences. This supports the need to accommodate the processes of blending and merging of cultural knowledge into a living and organic outcome within the processes of museology and cultural heritage practice.

The RKS led the project with a clear sense of ownership, and through a series of community consultations, they developed collective agency. In part this was achieved through adopting a people-centred approach to heritage conservation, which gained authority and currency through the DU team and their understanding and association with the broader discourse of heritage management in Asia. The resulting framework created a new spatial domain that is the site for the expression of contemporary cultural activity and identity, and thus a resource for heritage conservation and cultural representation. In addressing these challenges, the concluding results from the five-year KHCMDP can be seen as seminal; establishing the foundational philosophies based on sound academic principles, contemporary museological, heritage and design practices to make solid progress towards a sustainable project.

We can learn from this project and apply this knowledge to future projects. Primarily cultural ownership must be maintained by the community, and the final outcomes must be managed by key stakeholders in the community. Academics entering into these relationships need to be aware of their own lack of agency, handing responsibility to others, and be patient in the outcomes as the community groups navigate their way to articulating their own identity. More importantly, the representation of that identity for an external audience is one to be negotiated in an ongoing process with Government patronage, external funding and internal navigation. The concluding result is not a clearly defined outcome but one where the foundations are established for the conversation to continue.

Although the development of the community museum presented some challenges, the KHCMDP can be deemed a highly successful collaboration. The completed building, a majestic representation of Kelabit culture sitting in a prominent position in the town of Bario, is a significant symbol of community agency that united the Kelabit as they addressed their heritage preservation. Through the KHCMDP, the Kelabit community may well be on their way to realising their ambitions – independently and despite the challenges – and provide a model of how an indigenous community can develop meaningful agency in the conservation and representation of their cultural heritage.

Notes

1 Carina Katigbak, Meghan Foley, Lauren Robert and M. Katherine Hutchinson, 'Experiences and Lessons Learned in Using Community-Based Participatory Research to Recruit Asian American Immigrant Research Participants', *Journal of Nursing Scholarship*, Vol.210, No.2, 2016, pp. 210–218, p. 214.
2 S. Robert Aiken and Colin H. Leigh, 'Seeking Redress in the Courts: Indigenous Land Rights and Judicial Decisions in Malaysia', *Modern Asian Studies*, Vol.45, No.4, July 2010, pp. 825–875, pp. 832–833.
3 Richard Sandell, *Museums, Society, Inequality*, Routledge, London, 2002, p. 7.
4 Cecilia Sman, 'Teripun a Reminder of Kelabits' Roots', *Borneo Post Online*, 14 August 2016, www.theborneopost.com/2016/08/14/teripun-a-reminder-of-kelabits-roots/, accessed 18 July 2017.
5 Ibid, 2016.

Index

action research 4–5, 89–90, 102
Ahearn, Laura 64
Ahmad, Abu Talib 3
Aiken, S. Robert 7, 10–11, 121
Alivizatou, Marilena 38
Amster, Matthew 8
Anderson, Benedict 7
Ang, Susan 96, 102
anthropology 25, 38
Anvi, T.K. 37
architecture 5, 19, 25, 88, 91–92, 95, 101–102, 105–106, 108, 110
Asia Indigenous People Pact (AIPP) 9, 10
Association of Southeast Asian Nations (ASEAN) 12
Australia Malaysia Institute (AMI) 108
authenticity 1, 14, 27–28, 45–46, 49–51, 54, 60, 65–66, 70, 114, 116, 118

Bala, Poline 8, 40, 74
Bandarin, Francesco 58
Banks, Edward 23, 78
Baram 7, 10, 75
Baram District Council 10, 96
Baram River 6, 14, 34, 36
Bario 6, 9–11, 14, 23–24, 33, 35–37, 41–42, 46–48, 52–53, 61, 73–74, 77–78, 84–85, 88, 91–92, 95–100, 102, 105–108, 112, 120–122, 125
Bario Asal 36, 41, 46–47, 60–61, 72, 75, 121–122
Bario Nukenan (Food) Festival 12
Barisan Nasional (BN) 10
Barker, Graeme 78

Batu Lawi 14, 107–108, 123
Berma, Madeline 52
Bin Keromo, Paiman 65
biodiversity 67, 76–77
Borneo 1, 6–8, 12–14, 22–23, 25, 34–36, 39–40, 46, 53, 57, 60–61, 66–67, 76–77, 85, 87, 101
Borneo Evangelical Mission 7
Borneo International Beads Conference 40
Borneo Research Bulletin 33
Borneo Research Council 76
Bowers, John 39
branding 88, 92, 95, 100, 107–108
branding strategies 107
British Colony 8, 23, 34, 36, 40, 60, 72
Brooke 22–23, 25
Brooke, Charles 22
Brooke, James 22
Brookes Dynasty 34
Brosius, J. Peter 66–67
Brunei 3, 37, 76–77
built environment 47, 88, 100, 102
Bulan, Lucy 25, 33, 73–74
Bulan, Ramy 74, 77
bumiputera 7
Burdick, Jake 88
Burn, Dennis 2

capacity building 1, 86, 88, 97, 117, 119
Chapman-Walker, John 36
Chin, Lucas 26, 40–41
Chong, Jinn Winn 46
christian 7–8, 10, 15, 32, 47, 58, 71–74, 116, 124

christianity 5, 7–8, 15, 33, 39, 41, 70, 72, 74, 102–104, 115
Clifford, James 19
Coates, Rebecca 42
collective community agency 64
Colombo Plan 73
colonial museum 13, 19–21, 25
community consultation 5, 10, 29, 37, 63, 86, 88, 91, 95, 98–99, 102–103, 105–106, 113, 115–116, 118, 120, 123–124
community engagement 59, 79, 99–100, 124
community participation 5, 12, 14, 20, 86, 88, 105, 107, 123
Confrontation (the) 11, 71, 73–74, 105–106, 121
conservation practitioners 1, 28
Cooper, Dave 40
cross-cultural 15, 86–87, 89, 91, 96
cultural centre 12–13, 15, 29, 48, 64, 114, 116–117, 123
cultural democracy 52, 115–116
cultural development 13, 15, 36, 38, 53, 122
cultural diversity 1, 2, 83
cultural heritage management 86
cultural hybridity 29, 73, 115, 124
cultural knowledge 124
cultural landscape 2, 11, 66, 74, 78–79, 122
cultural representation 1, 5–6, 13, 26, 45, 49, 57–58, 63, 81, 87, 102, 114, 116–117, 119, 123–124
cultural tourism 13
Curtis, Kimberley 89

Davis, Peter 63
Dayak 24, 51
Dayak Cultural Foundation (DCF) 51–52
Deakin University 15–16, 65, 83–84, 86–89, 90–92, 95–97, 99–102, 106, 107–108, 110, 119, 121–122, 124
decolonisation 1, 3, 5, 19, 61, 71–72, 82
Dellios, Paulette 49–50
design 2, 5, 19, 25, 29, 34, 38, 47–48, 61, 65, 74, 81–83, 88–92, 95–97, 99–101, 104–108, 110–112, 115, 118–124
digital 100
diverse origins 1
diversity 1, 10, 23, 46, 50, 53, 63, 65, 83, 90–91
Doering, Zahava 111
Durrans, Brian 61

East Malaysia 3, 6, 13–14, 46, 61
Eaton, Peter 76
eBario 5, 84, 87
ecomuseums 58–59, 63, 65
economic development 2, 3, 5, 13–14, 45, 48, 52, 67, 78, 90
ecotourism 10, 53
environmental conservation 76
ethnic identity 114
ethnicity 1, 7, 15, 25
Ewart, Ian 47
exhibition 21, 37–39, 49, 52, 92, 95, 99–100, 105, 108, 110–113, 117, 123–124
exhibition design 19, 100, 108
experiential learning 89, 97

fieldwork 33, 99, 111
food festival 12, 48, 52
funding 72, 85, 92, 99, 101, 108, 124–125

Gala, Garawat 10
Galla, Amar 86
Giroux, Henry 88
Gomes, Alberto 54
Gunung Mulu National Park 77

Haddon, A.C. 37
Harris, Roger W 48, 84
Harrisson, Barbara 24
Harrisson, Tom 23–26, 34–41, 61, 71–72, 75, 78
Hazelius, Artur 59
headhunting 35, 104, 106
Heart of Borneo 53, 77
Heiman, Judith M 23
heritage conservation 1–2, 5–6, 12–13, 20, 26–29, 36, 47–48, 51, 54, 57, 63, 65, 79, 114, 116, 122–124

Index

heritage interpretation 35, 42, 74, 95, 108, 118
heritage making 5, 7, 28, 38, 62, 67, 71, 73–74, 76, 81, 89, 114, 116–117
Hewitt, John 22
Hill, Jane 64
Hill, Lara 53
Hoi An Protocol 27, 65
Hong, Evelyne 14
Hose, Charles 40, 60, 61
human rights 1, 2
Huxley, Julian 39
hybrid 8, 16, 24, 28–29, 46, 60, 81, 124
hybridity 29, 32, 73, 115, 124

Iban 23, 25, 34, 40, 51–52, 75
identity 3, 7–9, 13–14, 28, 32, 34–35, 45–46, 57–58, 64, 66, 70–75, 78, 81–83, 92, 95–96, 114–115, 123
Indian Museum, Calcutta 21, 22
indigenous knowledge 1, 14, 24, 57, 66–67, 83, 87
indigenous knowledge systems 27, 66, 114, 117
Indonesia 6, 14, 22, 46, 53, 71, 74, 77, 121
intangible heritage 36–39, 60, 83, 88, 100, 114, 12
International Centre for the Study of the Preservation and Restoration of Cultural Property (ICCROM) 12, 20, 26–27, 65, 95
International Council of Museums (ICOM) 12, 20, 26, 96
International Islamic University, Malaysia 101
interpretation 25, 35–38, 42, 46, 53, 58, 64, 67, 70, 74, 81, 88, 92, 95, 98–100, 104, 108, 111, 118, 123
interpreting history 106
Irvine, Judith 64
Islam 10, 15, 20

Jala, Idris 10
Janowski, Monica 61–62
Jansen, Father Henry 8
Japanese 22–23, 34–35
Kalimantan 14, 22, 75–76, 107
Keat Gin, Ooi 72–73
Kebing, Nelson 108

Kelabit Culture 28, 32, 34, 36–38, 47–48, 58, 60–62, 67, 71, 78, 97, 104–105, 115, 119, 121, 125
Kelabit Highlands 3, 6, 8, 10, 12–13, 15–16, 23, 25, 32–34, 36, 38, 41, 46–48, 53–54, 61, 66–67, 71, 75–78, 81, 84–85, 87, 95–96, 99, 107, 109, 112, 114, 116–117, 122
Kelabit identity 11, 13, 16, 35, 47–48, 107, 110–111, 113, 115–116, 122, 124
Kelabit language 24, 60, 107, 118
Kelly, Meghan 96, 100, 102, 108
Kenyah 76
Kreps, Christina 57, 63, 107
Kress, Gunther 84
Kuala Lumpur 7, 21, 45, 119
Kuching 6–7, 13, 21–24, 36, 39–40, 71, 98, 100, 108, 119, 121

Labang, David 24, 33
Latrell, Craig T 50–51
Lave, Jean 64
Legend of Tuked Rini 62
Leigh, Colin H 7, 10–11, 121
Lenzi, Iola 45
Lian, Robert 33
longhouse 8–9, 11, 14, 24–25, 33–37, 40–41, 46–47, 52–53, 60–63, 66, 73–75, 78, 91, 96, 98, 104–108, 117, 119, 121–123
Lowenthal, David 7
Lugun, Isaac 71, 74, 85, 100
Lugun, Nikki 48, 71, 74, 83–85, 87

MacKenzie, John 21
Mahmud, Abdul Taib 10
Maitland, Gary 22
Malaysia 1–4, 6–7, 9–15, 19–21, 27–29, 32, 39–40, 45–46, 49–51, 53–54, 57–58, 61, 65, 71–75, 77, 79, 82, 85, 87, 91, 96, 98, 101, 108, 114–115, 121
Malaysian Federation 72–73, 75
Malaysian Tourism Promotion Board 50
Malaysia's Vision 2020 52
Malinowski, Bronislaw 38–39
material culture 25, 32–33, 36–37, 42, 45, 59, 107
McDonald Institute for Archaeological Research, University of Cambridge 77

McKeich, Cherie 21
Metcaff, Peter 35
Ministry of Culture, Arts and Tourism (MOCAT) 51
Miri 6, 8, 10, 53, 77, 91–92, 98, 100, 103, 105, 119–121
Missionaries 7, 8, 72
modernity 5, 8, 15, 24, 28, 48, 70, 74
Molton, John 22
Morrison, Hedda 41, 61
Mukhaji Bengali T. N. 21
Mulu World Heritage Area 53
museology 5, 12, 14, 19–20, 23, 25, 29, 45, 57, 66, 82, 95–96, 115, 124
museum studies 1, 12, 88, 97, 108, 110
Muslim 3, 7, 15, 45–46
musyawarah 9
Mutang Urd, Anderson 76

native customary lands 75
Nederveen Pieterse, Jan 29
Ngidang, Dimbab 66

O'Malley, Michael P 88
Operation SEMUT 23
Orang Asli Museum, Kuala Lumpur 45
Osman, Sabihah 9, 75

Pa Bengar 37
Pa Lungun 37
Pa'Dalih 62
Paran, Walter 42
participatory action research 4, 89–90, 102
Pelaba, Balang 62
Penan 35, 67, 75–76
penghulu 9
Perak State Museum, Malay Peninsula 21
Phoa, John 75
policy development 99
Presta Nukenen (Food Festival) 48
Pringle, Robert 34
public pedagogy 88–89
Puyok, Arnold 10

radio Bario 53
Raffles Museum, Singapore 21
Rainforest World Music Festival 49
Raja, Leila Hodder 53

Reitsma, Elizabeth Simone 82, 83
representation 1, 4–7, 11–16, 19–22, 25–26, 28–29, 32–33, 40, 45–47, 49–52, 54, 57–59, 61, 63, 66–67, 70, 81–83, 87–88, 92, 97–98, 100, 102, 105, 107, 112–117, 119–120, 122–125
Riveire, George Henri 59
Roman Catholic Mission 41
Rubenstein, Carol 24
Rurum Kelabit Sarawak (RKS) 9–11, 15, 19–20, 24–26, 29, 32, 40, 45, 48–49, 53–54, 57–58, 62–63, 70–77, 83–87, 90–92, 95–101, 106–108, 115–117, 119–124
Russell-Cook, Myles 82
Rutter, Owen 40, 42

Saba 41
Saging, Robert 33
Sandell, Richard 54, 123
Sandin, Benedict 25
Sandlin, Jennifer 88
Sarakraf 39
Sarawak 1–4, 6–11, 13–15, 20–29, 32–34, 36, 38–40, 45, 49–52, 60–61, 66–67, 71–76, 78, 82, 84, 86, 88–89, 100, 114–115, 121
Sarawak Cultural Village, Kuching (SCV) 49–52, 108
Sarawak Economic Development Corporation 39 49
Sarawak Information Service 73
Sarawak Land Code 75
Sarawak Land Consolidation and Rehabilitation Authority (SALCRA) 75
Sarawak Museum, Kuching 21–25, 33, 36, 39–40, 61, 86, 107, 114
Sarawak Museum Journal (SMJ) 24–26
Schneeberger, Werner F 34
Selangor Museum, Kuala Lumpur 21
Shelford, Robert 61
social development 5, 11–13, 48, 59, 74, 85, 87, 121
socioeconomic development 64
Southwell, Hudson 8
Sweet, Jonathan 59, 84, 86, 95, 96–97, 100, 107–108

tangible heritage 77
Tarawe, John 10, 53, 96–97
Tarawe, Lian 108, 109
Teripun Tauh 107
tourism 2, 14–15, 24, 38–40, 45–46, 48, 51–54, 65, 76, 83–84, 86–87, 99, 101, 105, 110, 115–116, 122
Tourism Malaysia 51
traditional knowledge 26, 38–39, 48, 53, 60, 65–66, 70, 117
traditional knowledge systems 115
traditional values 47, 116

UNESCO 1–2, 12, 20, 25–28, 39, 58, 65, 77, 95–96
UNESCO Convention for the Safeguarding of the Intangible Cultural Heritage 83

UNESCO Indigenous Arts Program 39
UNESCO World Heritge 1, 77
University of Malaysia, Sarawak 40, 74, 77

visual communication 5, 96, 104, 106–108, 110–111

Walker, Paul 19
Wallace, Alfred Russell 22
Wenger, Etienne 64
Wills, Jo 59
Wilmot, Simon 96–98, 101
WWII 3, 5, 7, 19, 21–23, 28–29, 32–36, 41, 57, 60–62, 70–72, 74, 102, 106, 115

Yong, Tan Tai 3